Contents

6	The Success of Insects
6	The Value of Insects
7	What Is an Insect?
9	The Life Cycle of Insects
9	Insect Senses

Non-Insects

11	Scorpions
12	Daddy-longlegs or Harvestmen
13	Mites
14	Ticks
15	Spiders
16	Black Widow
17	Tarantulas
18	Orb-weavers
19	Jumping Spiders
20	Sowbugs
21	Millipedes
22	Centipedes
23	Springtails

Insects

(listed in order from primitive to advanced)

24	Twintails
24	Humpbacked Bristletails
26	Silverfish
27	Mayflies
28	Dragonflies and Damselflies
29	Roaches
30	Termites
32	Mantises
32	Zoraptera
34	Ice Crawlers
35	Earwigs
36	Stoneflies
37	Migratory Locusts
39	Katydids
39	House Crickets
40	Walkingsticks and Leaf Insects
41	Webspinners
42	Booklice and Barklice
43	Lice
44	Thrips
45	Bugs and Their Allies
46	Backswimmers
47	Giant Water Bugs
48	Water Striders
49	Bed Bugs
50	Plant Bugs
51	Assassin Bugs
52	Lace Bugs
53	Stink Bugs or Shield Bugs

54	Periodical Cicadas	80	Dance Flies
55	Treehoppers	81	Long-legged Flies
57	Spittlebugs or Froghoppers	82	Flower Flies
57	Leafhoppers	83	Fruit Flies
58	Fulgorid Planthoppers	84	Vinegar Flies
59	Jumping Plantlice	85	House and Stable Flies
60	Whiteflies	87	Tsetse Flies
61	Aphids or Plantlice	87	Blow Flies
62	Mealybugs and Scale Insects	88	Flesh Flies
63	Dobsonflies and Alderflies	89	Tachina Flies
64	Lacewings and Antlions	90	Bot and Warble Flies
65	Green Lacewings	91	Caddisflies
66	Antlions	92	Moths and Butterflies
67	Snakeflies	93	Ghost Moths and Swifts
68	Scorpionflies	94	Clothes Moths and Their Allies
69	Fleas	95	Bagworm Moths
70	Two-winged Flies	96	Clearwing Moths
71	Crane Flies	97	Gelechiid Moths
72	Mosquitoes	99	Codling Moths
73	Midges	99	Spruce Budworms
75	Biting Midges	100	Pyralid Moths
75	Black Flies	101	Plume Moths
76	Gall Midges	102	Geometrid Moths
76	Horse and Deer Flies	102	Silkworm Moths
78	Robber Flies	104	Tent Caterpillar Moths
79	Bee Flies	105	Tussock Moths

A BANTAM NATURE GUIDE

KNOWLEDGE THROUGH COLOR

INSECTS OF THE WORLD

BY JEANNE E. REMINGTON

A RIDGE PRESS BOOK/BANTAM BOOKS
TORONTO   NEW YORK   LONDON

Photo Credits

BC—Bruce Coleman
LR—Luisa Ricciarini
NA—National Audubon Society
PM—Pictor Milano
PR—Photo Researchers
TS—Tom Stack & Associates

Archivio Foto B: 126, 127; Archivio Fotografico Longo: 61, 154; Ron Austing (BC): 54 (rt.), 63 (tp.); E. S. Barnard (BC): 105 (tp. & btm. left); J & D Bartlett (BC): 111 (left); Gary Bernard: 10, 80, 81; Carlo Bevilacqua: 29 (rt.), 33 (tp.), 40 (btm.), 121, 130 (tp.), 137 (rt.),149; S. C. Bisserot (BC): 64, 66 (tp.), 109; Alan Blank (BC): 47; Jane Burton (BC): 48; Center for Disease Control: 43; J.A.L. Cooke (BC): 12 (tp.), 27 (tp.), 105 (rt.); H. N. Darrow (BC): 70 (btm. left), 115 (tp.), 117 (tp.), 120 (tp. left & btm. rt.); Treat Davidson (NA): 94; E. R. Degginger (TS): 45, 51 (tp.), 53, 54 (left), 56 (btm. left), 89, 100, 145 (rt.); A. J. Dignan (BC): 85 (btm. rt.); W. & M. Epping (PM): 146; foto Bucciarelli: 25 (tp.), 29 (left), 30 (rt.), 31 (btm.), 36 (btm.), 55, 86 (tp.), 101, 118, 132, 136, 139; Neville Fox-Davies (BC): 112; Donato Giussani (LR): 19, 25 (btm.), 26, 51 (btm.), 70 (rt.), 79, 95, 123, 129, 131, 145 (left); Bob Gossington (BC): 16, 125 (mid.); Ted Gruen (BC): 147 (rt.); Wally Guy (U.S. Forest Service): 98 (btm.); W. Harstrick (PM): 27 (btm.), 65, 77 (btm.), 128; G. E. Hyde (BC): 103 (tp.), 111 (tp. & btm. rt.); 120 (tp. rt.), 144; Bill Noel Kleeman (TS): 155 (left); John Kohout (TS): 107; K. Kohout (TS): 56 (mid.); W. Kratz (PM): 18, 21, 38 (tp.), 68, 71, 78, 86 (btm.), 98 (tp.), 104, 133, 138; Aldo Margiocco: 119, 152 (tp.); Giuseppe Mazza: 11, 13, 20, 22, 28 (btm.), 30 (left), 31 (tp.), 35, 37, 40 (tp.), 46, 56 (tp. left & rt.), 60, 62 (tp. left), 67, 82, 84, 88, 92, 103 (btm. left & rt.), 110, 114, 122, 137 (left), 140; Migale (PM): 17; W. J. C. Murray (BC): 93; Tom Myers (TS): 7, 36 (tp.), 38 (btm.), 76, 115 (btm.), 117 (btm. rt.); Oxford Scientific Films (BC): 62 (rt.), 135; F. Park (PM): 117 (btm. left); R. E. Pelham (BC): 62 (btm. left); Pictor Milano: 72, 73, 151; Louis Quitt (PR): 77 (rt.); David C. Rentz (BC): 34 (tp.); Carl W. Rettenmeyer: 12 (btm.), 56 (btm. rt.), 58 (tp. left), 63 (btm.), 70 (tp. left), 85 (btm. left), 148, 150 (tp.), 157; Harry Rogers (PR): 69, (NA): 141 (tp. left); E. S. Ross: 33 (btm.), 34 (btm.), 41, 42 (btm.), 44, 49, 50, 58 (tp. rt. & btm.), 59, 66 (btm.), 74, 83, 85 (tp.), 90, 91, 96, 103 (mid.), 106, 108, 125 (tp. & btm.), 130 (btm.), 134, 141 (tp. rt. & btm. left), 142 (tp.), 143, 147 (left), 150 (btm.), 155 (rt.), 156; F. Sauer (PM): 14, 15; G. Tomsich (LR): 28 (tp.); M. W. F. Tweedie (BC): 23, 42 (tp.), 52, 142 (btm.), 152 (btm.), 153; U.S.D.A.: 97; Helmut Wolf (PM): 113
Front Cover (Bumble Bee): Bill Noel Kleeman (TS)
Title Page (Skipper Butterfly): Tom Myers (TS)
Back Cover (Giant Water Bug): Alan Blank (BC)
Drawings: Denis Prince

INSECTS OF THE WORLD

A Bantam Book published by arrangement with The Ridge Press, Inc.
Text prepared under the supervision of Laurence Urdang Inc.
Designed and produced by The Ridge Press, Inc. All rights reserved.
Copyright 1975 in all countries of the International Copyright Union
by The Ridge Press, Inc. This book may not be reproduced in whole or in part
by mimeograph or any other means, without permission. For information
address: The Ridge Press, Inc., 25 West 43rd Street, New York, N.Y. 10036.
Library of Congress Catalog Card Number: 74-19830
Published simultaneously in the United States and Canada.

Bantam Books are published by Bantam Books, Inc.
Its trademark, consisting of the words "Bantam Books" and the portrayal
of a bantam, is registered in the United States Patent Office
and in other countries. Marca Registrada
Bantam Books, Inc., 666 Fifth Avenue, New York, N.Y. 10019
Printed in Italy by Mondadori Editore, Verona.

106	Noctuid Moths	133	Soldier Beetles
107	Underwing Moths	134	Fireflies or Lightning Beetles
108	Tiger Moths	135	Dermestid Beetles
109	Giant Silkworm Moths	136	Blister Beetles
110	Luna Moths	137	Darkling Beetles
111	Sphinx Moths	138	Lady Beetles
112	Giant Skipper Butterflies	139	Longhorned Beetles
113	Skippers	140	Leaf Beetles
114	Whites and Sulphurs	141	Weevils
115	Swallowtails	142	Bark Beetles
116	Viceroys	143	Twisted-wing Insects
116	Monarchs	144	Wasps, Bees, and Ants
118	Satyrs and Wood Nymphs	145	Sawflies
119	Morpho Butterflies	146	Ichneumon Wasps
120	Blues, Coppers, and Hairstreaks	147	Gall Wasps
121	Beetles	148	Fig Wasps
122	Tiger Beetles	149	Spider Wasps
123	Ground Beetles	150	Velvet Ants
124	Predacious Diving Beetles	151	Yellowjackets and Hornets
124	Whirligig Beetles	152	Hunting Wasps
126	Water Scavenger Beetles	153	Leafcutter Bees
127	Rove Beetles	154	Honey Bees
128	Carrion Beetles	155	Bumble Bees
129	Stag Beetles	156	Ants
130	Scarab Beetles	157	Army Ants
131	Flatheaded Borers	158	Index
132	Click Beetles		

Introduction

The Success of Insects
Insects are the most successful animals that have ever evolved. They were among the first on earth (long before dinosaurs or flowering plants) and have been around ever since—probably about 400 million years.

Flourishing in ice ages as well as periods of heat, they have expanded and diversified so astoundingly that now they make up more than three-fourths of known animal species! Over 900,000 species are already named and many more are discovered each year. Contrast this with the known species of birds (8,600) or even the number of all vertebrates from fishes to man (60,000).

Extinction is not a fate facing the group in the predictable future, for their reproductive capacities and tremendous diversity allow them to adapt to environmental changes. Pollution, overcrowding, limited food, elimination of habitats—all can be coped with by many kinds of insects. An outstanding example of this is the resistance to certain insecticides that quickly evolved in successive generations of mosquitoes, lice, and aphids.

Almost everywhere one can find insects, from mountain heights to seashores, tundra to tropics, even in hot springs and glaciers. Only the sea is free from mass invasion: just a few insects survive in or on it. Examples of the fantastic diversity of insect appearance, habits, and life histories can be seen in the main part of this book.

The Value of Insects
Some insect products are of great value to humanity, honey and silk being the best-known examples. Other useful insect substances are wax (from bees), lac (from certain scale insects and used in shellac), and dyes. Jewelers and craftspeople make use of colorful beetle wing-covers and iridescent butterfly wings. As part of our natural environment, insect beauty, songs, and fascinating ways give us pleasure.

The most useful activity of insects is pollination of flowers, a necessity for the production of seeds. About half of all insects perform another vital role by eating or parasitizing other insects. Scavenging insects

Orb-weaver Spider wrapping Honey Bee

return dead plants and animals to the soil; other beneficial insects destroy noxious weeds.

A little-advertised value of insects is as human food. Insect eggs, soft immatures, and crunchy pupae provide essential and easily obtained protein and fats for primitive peoples today just as they have far back into earliest human history.

The destructive aspects of insects are too well known to dwell on—everyone is aware of the biters, stingers, infesters, parasites, disease-carriers, and crop-destroyers. But the vast majority of insects neither helps nor harms people nor their domestic animals nor cultivated plants. They are simply there, tiny but vital links in the web of life, providing indispensable food for fish, birds, and many other coexisters on this earth.

What Is an Insect?

Insects fit into the animal kingdom in the following ways: (1) they are invertebrates (animals without backbones); (2) among the divisions of invertebrates they belong to the major group Arthropoda, meaning "jointed legs." All arthropods have an external skeleton that is divided into segments or rings, some of which bear pairs of jointed appendages. Other common arthropods are horseshoe crabs, spiders, scorpions, ticks, centipedes, millipedes, and crustaceans (crayfish, lobsters, crabs, and sowbugs).

Adult insects differ from all other arthropods in having:
1) A body divided into three parts—head, thorax, and abdomen.
2) One pair of antennae.
3) Three pairs of legs.
4) Wings. Not all insects have wings but all winged invertebrates are insects. A few kinds of insects have become secondarily wingless or legless because of their habitat or activities, and the three most primitive and ancient orders of insects (silverfish, twintails, and humpbacked bristletails) have never had wings in their long evolutionary history.

General Form of an Insect

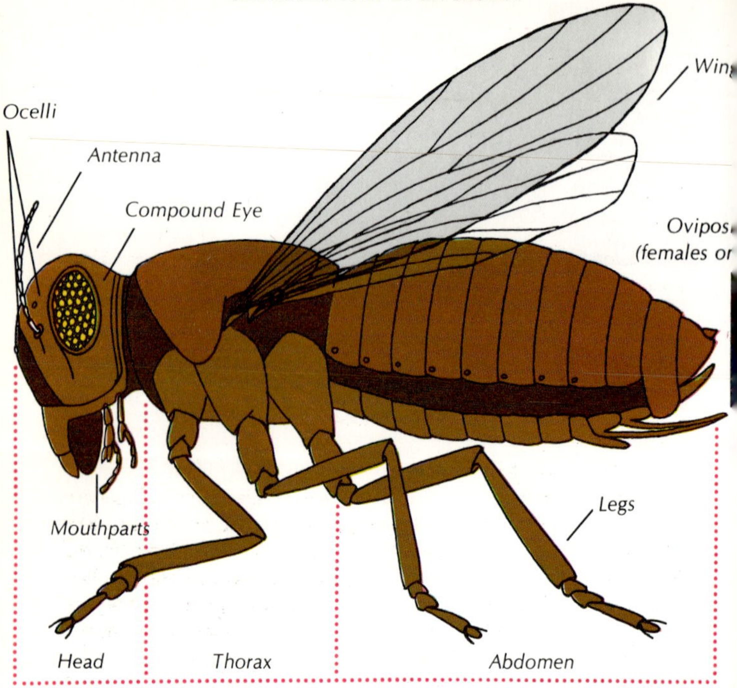

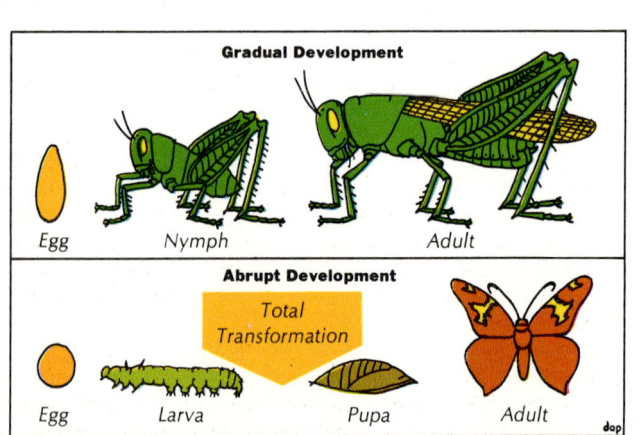

- Ocelli
- Antenna
- Compound Eye
- Wing
- Ovipos (females or
- Mouthparts
- Legs
- Head
- Thorax
- Abdomen

Gradual Development

Egg — Nymph — Adult

Abrupt Development

Egg — Larva — Total Transformation — Pupa — Adult

The outer covering or shell of an insect is its skeleton, providing structural strength and anchorage for muscles. It also protects the internal tissues and keeps them from drying out. The shell cannot expand so it must be split and shed from time to time as the insect grows. This process is called *molting*. Before each molt the insect develops a soft, new, and larger (though slightly compressed) shell inside the old one; after the molt the new one expands and hardens.

The Life Cycle of Insects

The change in form during growth is called *metamorphosis*. There are two general styles of insect metamorphosis: gradual and abrupt. The young of insects with the gradual type are frequently called *nymphs*. Right from the beginning, on hatching from the egg, nymphs look like their parents, except that they are smaller and lack reproductive organs and wings. The nymphs grow gradually; like mammals, they change proportions but not form. Part way through this development the future wings appear as small pads and get larger with each molt. Gradual metamorphosis takes place in the first 19 insect orders, from twintails through bugs. Among the basically gradual types, the mayflies, dragonflies, damselflies, and stoneflies have nymphs with a specialized appearance because they are aquatic and therefore not very similar to their terrestrial parents.

In the insect orders with abrupt metamorphosis, the young do not resemble the adults at all and never have wing pads. There is a sudden change in most organs of the body when the larval tissues are extensively rebuilt into adult form at the time of pupation. The pupal period is a quiescent, non-feeding stage during which the newly created adult is firmed up preparatory to flying and mating. This type of metamorphosis is found in the 11 most advanced insect orders, from dobsonflies to bees, wasps, and ants.

Insect Senses

Insects have two kinds of eyes: compound and simple. A compound eye is made up of a number (from a few to thousands) of small individual

Close-up of compound eyes (Robber Fly)

lenses or facets clustered together like a honeycomb. Although this eye sees forms less well than a mammalian eye, it is better at detecting movement.

The primitive, simple eyes, or *ocelli,* form a group (usually three) on the front of the head. Each ocellus is a single, small lens perceiving light but not images. A few insects adapted for life in caves, soil, or other dark habitats have become eyeless.

Other insect senses are touch or vibration (detected by hairs or bristles all over the body, antennae, and legs) and hearing (sounds are received by a drum-like cavity with a thin membranous covering located on the front legs, thorax, or abdomen). Tastes and smells are perceived by *chemoreceptors* that respond to chemical compounds such as those in food plants. Chemoreceptors are also important in sensing the chemical substances used by insects to communicate sexual attraction, alarm, socialization, and other signals. The antennae, feet, and other sites have chemoreceptors. All these sensory organs connect with the brain and nervous system.

Note: A majority of orders and families of insects may be found in most parts of the world. Usually there are more species and more individuals in warmer regions. Only the exceptions to these two rules are noted in this book.

The Class Insecta, like other animal classes, is divided into a number of orders. The orders are divided into families, the families into genera, and the genera into species. In the following pages the insects are described primarily on the order and family level because non-specialists recognize *types* rather than individual species—for example, dragonflies instead of any particular species of dragonfly.

Non-Insects

Scorpions
Class Arachnida, Order Scorpionida

Scorpions are unusual among arachnids: their young are born alive and carried about for a few days on the mother's back. Their mating is also exceptional—the male deposits a sperm sac on the ground, then takes hold of the female by her pincers in a kind of dance and maneuvers her into a position to accept the sac.

Like all arachnids, scorpions have no antennae, and the several small eyes are simple, not compound as in insects. Some African scorpions reach a length of 7 inches (18 cm) but the usual length is about 2½ inches (6.4 cm).

The "tail" is held in position for stinging enemies and sometimes for subduing the insects and spiders that are the food of scorpions. To humans, the sting of most scorpions is merely painful. However, there are a few species, especially in northern Mexico and northern Africa, that inject nerve poisons and cause many fatalities a year in rural areas where antidotes are not quickly available.

Daddy-longlegs or Harvestmen
Class Arachnida, Order Phalangiida

Eight very long, thread-like legs and a tiny round body suspended in the air above them identify the familiar daddy-longlegs. The legs are easily lost, but the animal is able to get along without one or two.

These harmless and slow-moving arachnids eat small insects, living or dead, but never become pests. They are not spiders and do not spin webs. Some have stink glands, which give off a liquid to repel enemies.

▲ *Megabunus diadema* ▼ Harvestman, Ecuador

Mites
Class Arachnida, Order Acarida

Though seldom seen by the average person, mites are extremely important and numerous. Many do serious economic damage to fruit and vegetable crops and ornamental plants; the "red spiders" on house plants are actually mites. The parasites, such as chiggers, burrow under the skin or feed externally on mammals, birds, and insects. Some of the animal parasites carry diseases, like scrub typhus. Mites occur in every environment: arctic, temperate, and tropical, and some even in salt water and hot springs.

Like the tick, a mite's body is a single unit, with no apparent neck or waist. Adults have eight legs, and there are no wings or antennae. Most mites are smaller than a pinhead, but some brightly colored ones may be as large as a lemon seed. "Beetle mites" superficially resemble tiny beetles and are scavengers in soil and under bark everywhere. They break down organic matter and thereby fertilize the soil. Many other kinds of mites have developed bizarre shapes which have been adapted for living on their hosts.

Ticks mating—bottom one bloated with blood

Ticks
Class Arachnida, Order Acarina

Ticks are external parasites of mammals, birds, or reptiles. They suck blood after thrusting the mouthparts through the skin of their hosts. After the meal, which may last several days, the ticks drop off, molt, then climb onto the tips of leaves of underbrush, to await a new host. One tick may have two or three hosts during its development. Although bereft of antennae or acute eyes, they sense when a host is near by detecting the exhaled carbon dioxide, whereupon they become very alert, waving their forelegs in the air. When the host brushes against them, they attach themselves. The eggs are laid in various places, but not on the host.

Several kinds of ticks are medically important because they transmit diseases such as relapsing fever, spotted fever, tularemia, and cattle fever.

Among the most familiar ticks are the wood ticks *(Dermacentor)* that infest humans in many parts of North America, and the brown dog tick *(Rhipicephalus sanguineus)*, which is cosmopolitan. The dog tick is often carried into houses on dogs, but it rarely bites people.

Jumping Spider

Spiders
Class Arachnida, Order Araneida

The most abundant arachnids except for the mites are the spiders, totaling about 30,000 species. They play an important role in the balance of nature by eating insects.

One of the reasons for the success of spiders is their ability to produce silk, a strong, elastic protein of many uses: to make webs for trapping prey, to provide shelter, to protect the eggs, and for the tiny young to "balloon" along on wind currents on a delicate strand of web. The silk is produced as a liquid in abdominal glands, spun out of tiny spinnerets below the back end of the body, and hardens as it comes into contact with the air. Production of this silk for commerce has not been feasible because spiders confined together tend to eat each other and cannot be mass-reared.

Spiders, like most arachnids, have two distinct body regions: the forepart, or cephalothorax, and the abdomen, joined by a narrow waist. The young resemble the adults, molting from a few to a dozen times as they outgrow their old skins. They have eight legs and eight simple eyes. Few spiders have poison dangerous to humans.

Black Widow
Latrodectus mactans

This dangerously poisonous spider lives in the warm parts of the world, but other widow spiders are found in colder climates. The female black widow builds her irregular web in dark niches under objects near buildings or dumps. She stays on her web, hanging upside down in the center, awaiting prey. The male wanders around looking for a mate, and he does not feed or bite. The female bites if molested, and the bite can cause severe abdominal and muscle pain.

Female black widows are about half an inch (13 mm) long; the male is smaller. Although the recognition mark of this species in most parts of the United States is the red hourglass on the underside of its abdomen, in other places the markings vary from irregular stripes to dots. The other species of widow spiders have various markings on a brown or gray background. Egg sacs also differ in appearance: the black widow's is brown and papery, the brown widow's is tufted, and the red widow's is white and smooth.

Tarantulas

Family Theraphosidae

This family contains the largest spiders, often called tarantulas in the United States, bird spiders in other places, and monkey spiders in South Africa. (The tarantula of the Mediterranean area is not in this group, but belongs to the wolf spider family.) The largest, a South American species, has a body 3½ inches (9 cm) long and a 10-inch (21 cm) leg span.

Most of these spiders live on the ground, a few in trees. They are nocturnal, hunting prey by sensing their vibrations. Insects are their usual diet but occasionally the large tarantulas capture a small snake, lizard, or nestling bird.

Tarantulas, except for a few kinds in Australia, are not dangerously poisonous to humans.

Large tropical tarantulas mature slowly, and the females may live as long as 20 years.

Orb-weavers
Family Araneidae

The classic spider web pattern seen in folk and fine arts is the type so elegantly crafted by orb-weavers—a spiral woven on strands radiating from the center and all in one vertical plane.

This family of about 2,500 species is worldwide. Their poor vision is compensated for by an acute sense of touch. When insect prey is caught in the web the orb-weaver rushes out, trusses the victim in strands of silk, and dissolves out its juices—spiders cannot swallow solid food.

In the summer or autumn each female produces egg sacs with several hundred eggs, which hatch in the fall or spring.

Jumping Spiders
Family Salticidae

Short-legged and agile, the tiny jumping spiders can pounce on insect prey from a distance many times their own length. They are daytime predators and have better eyesight than most other invertebrates. They are almost mammal-like in their alertness and behavior. No webs are woven but a strand of web is often used the way a mountain climber uses a rope.

This family includes the most colorful spiders, with beautiful patterns and some iridescence. Some of them resemble the color patterns of the flowers on which they lie in ambush, thus escaping the notice of unwary insect victims until it is too late. Jumping spiders are usually less than 7/10 inch (15 mm).

Most of the 2,800 species live in the tropics, but they are common in North America and Eurasia, too.

Sowbugs
Class Crustacea, Order Isopoda

The common garden sowbugs (also called woodlice or pillbugs) are sometimes mistaken for insects or millipedes. But they are crustaceans (like lobsters, shrimp, and crayfish). Sowbugs differ from insects in having 14 instead of just six legs.

These medium-sized, usually flattened animals have a shiny, hard covering over the back. The covering is divided into about 10 flexible plates, and some sowbugs, like armadillos, can roll up into a ball when disturbed.

Sowbugs are commonly found under stones, boards, and other debris, where they feed on decaying matter and fungi. They are usually harmless, but sometimes they damage the roots of cultivated plants.

Millipedes
Class Diplopoda

None of the "thousand-leggers"—as millipedes are sometimes called—really has a thousand legs. Most have fewer than 200. The newly hatched young may have as few as six legs, and more are added each time they molt until they mature. There are two pairs of legs on most segments of the long, cylindrical body. In spite of the many legs, millipedes move slowly. Some species roll up into a spiral or ball when disturbed.

Predators are repelled by a foul-smelling liquid which many millipedes exude from pores in the sides of the body. Millipedes live outdoors in damp, dark places such as leaf mold and rotting logs, and they feed on decaying plant matter. These animals cannot bite or sting. Rarely, they become pests in localized areas by feeding on living plants.

House Centipede

Centipedes
Class Chilopoda

"Hundred-leggers" are fast, active, nocturnal predators of insects and spiders, which they first paralyze with their poison fangs before eating. Centipedes are long and flat and have one pair of legs on each body segment. Most have fewer than 25 pairs, but the extremely long, slender kinds have many more.

The house centipede *(Scutigera coleoptrata)* is found in buildings in temperate climates and frequents damp places under sinks or tubs or around water pipes. It is harmless to humans and is probably mildly beneficial in eating pest insects, but it startles people because of its unusually long legs. Tropical centipedes (like *Scolopendra*) can be as long as 12 inches (30 cm) and can inflict painful bites.

Springtails
Order Collembola

These tiny arthropods have a forked spring on the underside of the abdomen that enables them to flip into the air when disturbed.

Springtails are often abundant on the surface of fresh water or sometimes on snow, when they are commonly called "snowfleas." Others live on the shores of oceans, lakes, and ponds, but most are in moist humus or soil. They are common on the soil of house plants, where they are quite harmless, but they can become minor pests of agricultural crops by feeding on germinating seeds or living plants, and they sometimes infest mushroom cultures. Usually they eat molds and decaying organic matter.

Springtails are wingless. Most have slender bodies but some are globular. They have prominent antennae but the eyes are missing or minute. Snowfleas are slate-colored while other springtails may be yellow, blue, brown, or white; some are mottled or patterned.

Although distributed worldwide, from pole to pole, springtails seem to be most plentiful in the cool, temperate regions.

Insects

Twintails
Order Entotrophi

Secretive creatures that live under rocks and logs, in plant litter and humus, or in deep caves, the Entotrophi are eyeless and wingless. Most are less than ¼ inch (6 mm) long, very slender, and whitish. They have two "tails," formed either into long filaments or into pincers. The segmented antennae look like strings of beads. Their mouthparts are mainly concealed by cheek folds, with only the tips protruding.

Most twintails supposedly feed on decaying plant material and fungi, but the pincer-bearers seize and eat insects and other arthropods. All are harmless to humans and of no economic importance. Some species live in groups. Mating does not involve copulation: the male deposits semen which the female takes into her genital opening. The eggs are laid in clumps, frequently on stalks, and some of the pincer-bearers guard both eggs and young.

Humpbacked Bristletails
Order Microcoryphia

Favorite haunts of these little-known insects are in needle litter beneath pine trees, on rocky coasts, and in lichen-covered stone walls. They hide by day and come out at night to feed on algae, lichens, and vegetable debris. The humpbacked bristletails, unlike their close relatives the silverfish, can jump with great agility by snapping the abdomen downward. Both groups molt continuously throughout their lives, and both have been wingless throughout their history.

These bristletails are soft-bodied, about ½ inch (13 mm) long, slender, and streamlined. They are covered with smoothly overlapping scales. The thorax is strongly humped and the head partly hidden under it. Both eyes and ocelli are large. Three long "tails," the middle one longest, project from the end of the body. On the underside of most abdominal segments are tiny pairs of rods, remnants of ancestral legs.

Mating is indirect: during courtship the male deposits a droplet of sperm suspended on a thread attached to the ground and sweeps it into the female's genital opening with his antennae. After fertilizing the eggs, she thrusts them into the soil, where they may overwinter. The nymphs take up to two years to mature.

▲ Twintail ▼ Humpbacked Bristletail

Firebrat

Silverfish
Order Thysanura

The silverfish, the most primitive of commonly seen insects, have probably existed with little change for over 300 million years.

Streamlined like a teardrop, wingless, and covered with dust-like slick scales, they vaguely resemble small flattened fish. Colors range from silvery to dark gray and from stripes to pinto blotches. They have three long tails, with the two side pieces held at right angles to the body. As is usual with insects, the long antennae and tails are loaded with delicate organs of touch and probably of taste and smell.

Most silverfish live outdoors and eat fungi and organic litter. A few inhabit buildings and feed on organic debris and starch, such as in stored books and clothing. One abundant household species around the world is the firebrat, which got its name from its preference for warm, moist areas around stoves, furnaces, and bakery ovens.

A small group lives in deep soil or caves and has lost eyes and the clothing of scales. Several others live only as "guests" in the nests of tropical ants or termites, where they steal food and speed away.

▲ Mayfly nymph ▼ Adult

Mayflies
Order Ephemeroptera

Swarms of mayflies in their aerial courtship and mating dance are a common sight near lakes and streams in warm weather. The three-tailed nymphs, which are flat, live in shallow fresh water, usually clinging to the undersides of stones. They are a major staple food of fish and are often used by anglers as bait.

Mayflies are soft-bodied and delicate, usually with three long tail filaments. They hold the two pairs of net-veined, clear wings together vertically over the back when not flying. The hind pair is much smaller than the front pair and is sometimes lost entirely.

Late in the final juvenile stage of the life cycle, the nymph leaves the water, the skin splits down the back, and the winged but sexually immature sub-adult emerges and makes a short flight. This stage is unique among insects because the mayfly molts once more after being able to fly. The adults mate, lay eggs, and die, all within a few hours or days. The fossil record of this conservative group goes back more than 300 million years.

Dragonflies and Damselflies
Order Odonata

These attractive insects are strong, agile fliers with sharp vision, and they grab their prey in flight. Their aquatic young are also predacious, catching their prey by whipping out a hinged mouthpiece, rather like toads and chameleons. Both groups benefit humanity by eating pest insects, and Odonata nymphs are an important fish food. Contrary to some myths, dragonflies and damselflies ("darning needles") are harmless to people: they cannot sting and do not bite.

Odonata have long, slender bodies, large heads, and enormous eyes. The four long, glassy wings look alike and have a dense network of veins. Dragonflies are larger and more robust than most damselflies and hold their wings outstretched when resting. In contrast, the damselflies close their wings together above the back.

The largest modern dragonfly has a 7½-inch (18 cm) wingspread; but dragonflies that lived 250 million years ago had wingspreads of at least 27 inches (70 cm)—the largest insects that ever lived.

▲ Dragonfly ▼ Damselfly

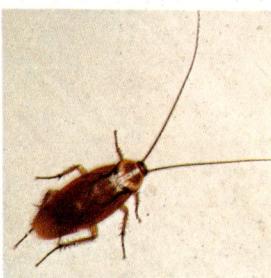

◀ *Blaberus giganteus*
▼ *Periplaneta americana*

Roaches
Order Blattaria

The majority of roaches live in the wild under logs, stones, or the bark of decaying trees. One kind can eat rotting wood and, like termites, has protozoans and cellulose-digesting bacteria in the intestines. Roaches are most abundant in the tropics. One of the largest living roaches (more than 2 inches or 50 mm long) is *Blaberus giganteus,* a native of the New World tropics.

Most roaches are swift runners, gregarious, and like warmth, humidity, and darkness. The several species that live in buildings hide by day and emerge at night to eat any organic matter they can find. *Periplaneta americana* is a worldwide species found in homes and other buildings, on ships, and in dumps. It is about 1¼ inches (30 mm) long.

The egg-laying roaches, such as *Periplaneta,* deposit batches of eggs in hard, symmetrical capsules, with the shape and sculpturing different for each species. *Blaberus* and other kinds bear the young alive and some even nourish the embryos with a structure similar to that of the human placenta. The life span of some roaches—four or five years—is unusually long for insects.

Numerous roach fossils have been found in 300-million-year-old rock formations.

Termites
Order Isoptera

Termites live in colonies, the only fully social insects outside of the ant, bee, and wasp group. They are falsely called "white ants," for they differ from ants in having (1) a broad "waist" at the junction of the thorax and abdomen, instead of a narrow, stem-like one; (2) workers with soft, pale bodies, instead of hard, dark ones; and (3) four wings of similar size rather than two large and two small.

The termite colony has three major castes: the reproductives, the workers, and the soldiers. All three include both sexes, but the latter two are sterile and permanently wingless. The winged reproductives swarm out of the nest at certain times and found new colonies. They soon shed their wings, and one pair becomes the king and queen, mate, and produce the future offspring of their own colony. A termite queen is the most prolific of insects: she can produce millions of eggs in her long lifetime (12 years or more). The workers do all the work except defense: they construct galleries, feed the colony, and care for the eggs. The soldiers have large, thickly armored heads and strong mouthparts, with which they attack intruders or plug up holes in the nest.

Termites live in tunnels and galleries in wood or soil, or in earthen mounds aboveground. Cellulose is their main food and is digested by special bacteria living in the intestinal tract. In the tropics termites perform a major role in converting dead trees into new soil.

The damp-wood termite is one of the most destructive North American insects. It lives in wood buried in soil or in contact with the soil, but always maintains tunnels to soil to get necessary moisture.

Huge pillar-like mounds up to 18 feet (5.5 m) high are the homes of the tropical mound-building termite. The mounds are composed of bits of earth, wood, and feces cemented together with termite saliva. The exterior is as hard as concrete. The interior is honeycombed with galleries and chambers in which fungi are cultivated for food.

Soldier Termite　　　　　　　　　　　　　Queens

▲ Mounds built by Tropical Termites ▼ Workers

31

Chinese Mantises
Order Mantodea

The Chinese mantis is native to Asia but was imported into northeastern North America around 1900 and is now common. It is 3 to 4 inches (83-104 mm) long. A similar though smaller species is native to Europe but is also abundant now in eastern North America.

Mantises help the balance of nature by eating other insects and occasionally even small frogs or lizards. The long spiny forelegs folded backward on themselves look as if they are in a praying position but the mantis is a deadly trap lying in wait for its prey. Due to a flexible "neck," the mantis is among the few insects that can look over their shoulders.

The female exudes a capsule of quick-drying brown froth containing 200 or more eggs and attaches it to a rock, plant, or tree. The young look like the adults except for size.

Mantises are very pugnacious, and in some species the female may eat the male during mating. In China, to provide amusement, two adult mantises were sometimes caged until they fought each other to death.

Zorapterans
Order Zoraptera

Rare and little known, the Zoraptera have only about 22 described species, the first having been discovered as recently as 1913.

Zorapterans are tiny (less than ⅛ inch, or 3 mm long). Their wings, which are eventually shed, are long, narrow, and transparent, with only one or two branched veins; the hind pair are smaller than the front ones. Some individuals never have wings and are blind, and the winged ones have both compound and simple eyes.

Although these tropical insects live in groups of up to 100 individuals, they have no caste system or division of labor. They live in dead wood, under bark, and in termites' nests, where they feed on fungi and mites.

▲ "Praying" Mantis ▼ Nymph Zorapteran

33

Ice Crawlers
Order Grylloblattodea

These rare, wingless insects are always found in mountains that are snow-covered most of the year. They prefer to be active at remarkably low temperatures, crawling about on soil or moss or under rocks at the edges of snow fields or glaciers. Dead organic matter seems to be their diet. Ice crawlers are difficult to find and are rare even in museum collections.

The pale body and antennae are long and slender, and there are two conspicuous tail filaments. The female uses her strong, sword-shaped ovipositor to lay eggs in the soil.

▲ Adult female ▼ Ice Crawlers mating in ice cave, California

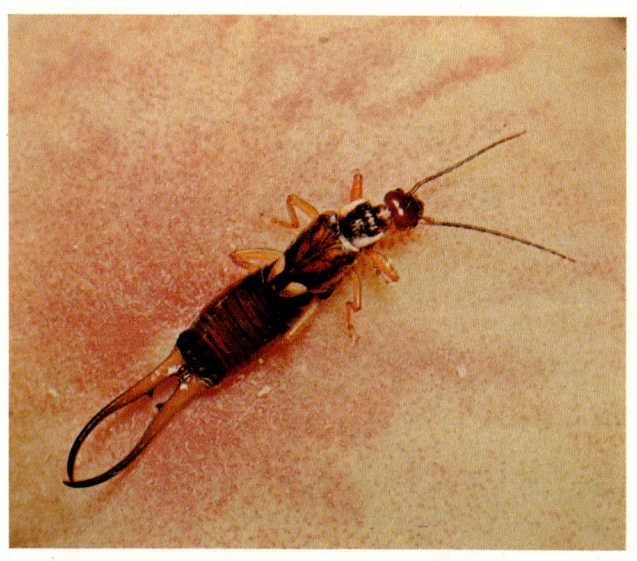

Earwigs
Order Dermaptera

The stout, shiny pincers at the end of the body are the outstanding feature of earwigs. The pincers are defensive weapons and perhaps are also used for folding up the fan-like hindwings. The short, leathery forewings cover all but the tips of the hindwings when not in flight.

Earwigs are nocturnal, living under stones, logs, and trash and feeding omnivorously on organic matter—vegetable or animal, living or dead. Several species live at the seashore. The female lays her eggs in soil or refuse and guards them until they hatch. These insects breed year round in the tropics, but in temperate climates there is one generation a year, with overwintering in the adult stage. Many are pests in farms, gardens, and houses.

▼ Stonefly adult ▲ Nymph

Stoneflies
Order Plecoptera

Stoneflies are among the most primitive of the winged insects. They are soft-bodied, seem to have no means of defense, and are usually drably colored to blend with their surroundings. They are poor fliers, seldom moving far from their breeding places. The short-lived adults feed little or not at all.

The aquatic nymphs, which molt between 30 and 40 times, crawl on the underside of submerged stones and debris in unpolluted streams and ponds and are one of the most abundant invertebrates in that habitat. Anglers use them for fish bait. Certain California Indians ate large stoneflies as a regular part of their diet, and the nymphs are eaten today (as are other aquatic insects) by people in many parts of the world.

Stoneflies have two pairs of equal, many-veined, glassy wings, which are folded flat on the back in repose, and a pair of tail filaments. The antennae are long and slender. Some northern hemisphere species are remarkable in their ability to emerge, mate, and lay eggs only in the coldest part of the winter.

Migratory Locusts
Order Orthoptera, *Family Acrididae*

Throughout human history migratory locusts have been feared and hated because of their devastation of agricultural crops. Recently scientists discovered that *crowding,* which induces physiological and behavioral changes in the locusts, triggers these massive migratory outbreaks: when the populations are dispersed and uncrowded the growing locusts develop into the "solitary phase," with pale color, slightly shorter wings, and no clustering; as the number of individuals builds up, darker and longer-winged locusts (the "migratory phase") are produced. Restless, hungry, strikingly social, they have a higher temperature, and bear more young. When the majority are of the crowded type, they swarm and migrate by the billions, traveling enormous distances. They may not eat much en route—their bodies have a high content of stored fat to sustain them—but once in a new area, they are insatiable, devouring vegetation down to the bare ground. There is normally at least a partial return migration, one generation moving westward, the next eastward.

Each continent except the polar regions has one or more species of migratory locust that at times reaches the swarming phase. The principal North American plague species, the Rocky Mountain locust, has not produced migrators during this century.

▲ Katydid ▼ House Crickets

38

Katydids
Family Tettigoniidae

Katydids are more often heard than seen. On warm late-summer evenings, males sit in fields and trees and produce "music" that is among the most pleasant of insect noises. As in crickets, the sounds are produced by rubbing a special scraper on one front wing against the file of the other. Each species of music-making Orthoptera has its own typical rhythm, with different signals for courting and fighting. The signals are heard by an eardrum (tympanum) on each front leg of crickets and katydids. In the Orient and occasionally in Europe, katydids, like songbirds, are kept in cages.

The very long, hair-like antennae, green, leaf-like appearance, and slightly flattened sides are typical of katydids. The females have large, sword-shaped ovipositors for inserting eggs, usually into plants.

As in other Orthoptera, the front wings are narrow and leathery and at rest cover the broad, thin, glassy hindwings, which are folded like fans along the sides of the body.

House Crickets
Family Gryllidae

The chirping "cricket on the hearth" of folksongs and tales has been introduced worldwide in human habitations; in the wild it lives solely in the Old World. It breeds continuously indoors, so any population may include individuals of all ages.

Females have long, awl-shaped ovipositors with which they thrust eggs into crevices (the outdoor denizens lay them in or on the ground). The eggs hatch in 15 to 25 days at 77°F (25°C) and the nymphs' development takes an equal amount of time.

Most crickets are nocturnal, starting to feed, drink, and court in late afternoon and continuing through the night. House crickets are omnivorous, feeding on any available organic matter, and may damage clothing, upholstery, and rugs.

Male crickets are extremely aggressive with each other and establish "peck orders" within their group by fighting. Although the combatants kick, wrestle, bite, and butt, there is rarely any physical damage done —the loser simply retreats. For a thousand years in the Orient, cricket fights have been staged for people to watch and wager on.

▼ Leaf Insect ▲ Walkingstick

Walkingsticks and Leaf Insects
Order Phasmatodea

If you see a stick or a leaf that moves on legs, you may be looking at one of nature's best examples of protective resemblance, a walkingstick or a leaf insect. The latter has a broad, leaf-like body and wings, and leaf-like extensions on the legs. Walkingsticks have a twig-like body and long, spindly legs. Both types are greenish or brownish and generally flightless and slow-moving, which helps them to escape the eyes of predators. For additional protection, some of these unusual insects can emit a foul-smelling liquid. Like many insects, if they are attacked and lose a leg, they are able to regenerate it, at least partly.

Walkingsticks live in trees or shrubs and feed on foliage. The seed-like eggs are dropped singly and fall to the ground, where they take one or two years to develop.

An adult of one species of tropical walkingstick is the longest insect on earth, reaching 13 inches (32 cm).

Webspinners
Order Embioptera

Silken tunnels spun by their own waving "hands" are home to the webspinners. The foreparts of the front legs are enlarged and contain the silk glands and spinnerets. The wingless females lay their eggs on the walls of the tunnels and show some parental care in tending the eggs and defending the newly hatched young.

The tunnels are found on grass or under stones, loose bark, or matted leaves. Although the webspinners live in large colonies, they don't have different working castes, as do the true social insects—the bees, ants, and wasps.

Less than ¼ inch (6 mm) long and very slender, these unusual insects can move rapidly and even run backwards. The winged males are also good fliers, with four long, membranous wings that look alike. They live in the tropics and subtropics and feed on dry plant material.

▲ Female adult ▼ Adult male with nymphs

Booklice and Barklice
Order Psocoptera

Booklice are minute, wingless insects that swarm on books and papers in dusty libraries and eat the starch on book bindings and page edges. But most members of this order live outdoors under bark or stones, on foliage, in bird nests, or in piles of dry grass. Organic debris, fungi, and lichens are their diet.

The booklice and barklice live only about two months, from hatching (from eggs covered with a silken network) to death. They are soft-bodied and pale, with long antennae. Most have two pairs of membranous wings, with the front pair much larger. Their size varies from less than 1/16 of an inch to ¼ inch (1-7 mm).

Some species become abundant in granaries, mills, and other buildings. Although they don't eat much of the stored cereal and grain, they contaminate it and make it unsaleable.

▲ Booklouse ▼ Barklouse

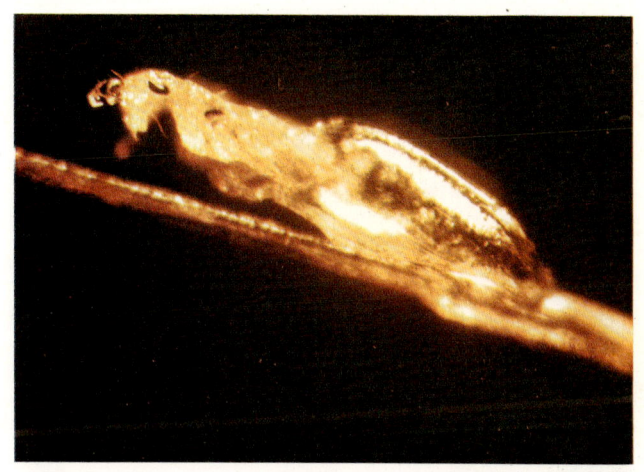

Louse emerging from egg

Lice
Order Phthiraptera

The human body louse or "cootie" has influenced the outcome of wars by spreading epidemics of typhus, trench fever, and relapsing fever among the armies. It is one of three species of lice that live on people, all of which are rare in uncrowded, sanitary environments: one lives on the head hair, one in seams and folds of clothing but crawls onto the skin to feed, and one on the pubic hair. Each stays within its own territory and is almost never found out of bounds. These lice pierce the skin and suck a little blood. Others, with chewing mouthparts, live mostly on birds and eat feathers, hair, and bits of dried blood and skin.

Lice live their entire lives on their hosts. The eggs are glued to the feathers or hair of the host or, in the case of the human body louse, to the clothing. The generations are continuous and overlapping, so the victim has no pest-free season.

The tiny, flattened, wingless bodies of lice, similar in young and adults, slide easily through the feathers or hair of the host aided by short, stout legs and claws. Lice are usually blind, or nearly so, and have very short antennae. Body lengths of sucking lice range from $1/12$ to $1/5$ inch (2-5 mm); chewing lice are slightly larger.

Thrips
Order Thysanoptera

If you pull apart wild daisies, you can usually see scurrying thrips. They are most abundant on plants and often seriously damage them while cutting plant tissues and sucking the juices. A few thrips eat fungi, dead plants, or are predators of mites and tiny insects.

The four narrow wings are thickly fringed with very long, hair-like bristles. The fringe closes up parallel to the wing margins when the wings are folded flat on the back.

Thrips have gradual metamorphosis and up to seven generations a year. The eggs are laid in plants or debris. Reproduction without fertilization of the eggs (parthenogenesis) is normal in some thrips, males of those species being rare or absent.

While moving from plant to plant thrips often pollinate flowers but they also carry plant diseases. Occasionally swarms of thrips are so thick that they fill the air over agricultural fields. On the whole, these tiny insects are more destructive than beneficial.

▲ Thrips in Morning Glory ▼ Nymphs on log

Giant Water Bug feeding on Mayfly nymph

Bugs and Their Allies
Order Hemiptera

The fifth largest order of insects, the Hemiptera comprise well over 50,000 species and about 150 families. It is a varied order, including both plant and animal feeders and a multitude of sizes, shapes, colors, habits, and environmental preferences.

The main shared feature is a long beak for piercing and sucking. Another is the gradual metamorphosis, sometimes quite complex. Most Hemiptera have four wings, large compound eyes, and short- or medium-length antennae.

In one of the two suborders of Hemiptera, the "true bugs," the forewings are "half-and-half"—that is, the front is leathery and opaque and the back is membranous; the hindwings are totally membranous. At rest the wings are folded flat on the back. (In the following pages the families from backswimmers through stink bugs are members of this group.) In the other suborder, the forewings are uniform throughout (either membranous or thickened) and at rest are held roof-like over the back. (The families from treehoppers through mealybugs have this type.)

Backswimmers
Family Notonectidae

The bugs that swim upside down can stay submerged for as long as six hours in cold weather, 30 minutes when warm, but then are forced to surface for air. One bubble of air is gathered between the wings and body and another among the interlocking hairs along the underside of the body. Their long, hair-fringed hindlegs are used like oars for swimming; the short forelegs are adapted for grasping prey.

Backswimmers live near the edges of ponds, lakes, and streams, hunting for the insects and crustaceans that are their main food. They also fly long distances and are often found around lights at night. Their eggs are laid on or in water plants or debris in the water. The young lead semi-aquatic lives like the adults, and both young and adults hibernate during the winter.

The back is often velvety and pale or mottled, which renders it less visible to aquatic prey and enemies looking upward; the ventral side is darker and duller. Body length is ⅛ to ⅝ inch (3-17 mm).

Young hatching from eggs glued to male's back

Giant Water Bugs
Family Belostomatidae

The largest of all Hemiptera are the giant water bugs. Some species reach a length of 4 inches (10.2 cm). Common in ponds and streams, these semi-aquatic insects feed on tadpoles, snails, frogs, small fish, and other insects. The prey is seized with the raptorial forelegs and the strong beak sucks out its juices. When picked up, giant water bugs can give humans a painful bite.

They swim with the four long, fringed hindlegs. Like many aquatic insects, they fly strongly, and frequently come to lights at night; they are sometimes called "electric-light bugs." Large Indo-Pacific species are eaten regularly by native peoples.

In some species of this family, the female glues the large eggs to the male's back, where they are carried around until hatching. The eggs of other species are dropped on the bottom of the pond or attached to water plants.

Giant water bugs are broad, brownish, and somewhat flattened. Their eyes cover most of the head and the bugs can easily see their prey when they are underwater.

Water Striders or Pond Skaters
Family Gerridae

The only truly marine insects—ones that spend their entire lives at sea far from land—belong to this family. They are species of the genus *Halobates* and live on the surface of tropical and subtropical oceans. Most water striders have wings, but during the evolution of sea-going *Halobates* the wings disappeared. The abdomen of *Halobates* also became smaller than that of its relatives, while the thorax became larger. The eggs of these saltwater striders are carried by the mother or deposited on floating seaweed or debris.

The two hind pairs of legs of water striders are extremely long and thin, ending in tufts of waterproof bristles that prevent the legs from breaking the surface film, permitting them to rest or to run with great agility over the water. Their bodies and legs, covered with a dense velvety pile, are also waterproof. The short front legs are used for grasping food: live insects or dead animal matter.

Most water striders live on fresh water but a few prefer brackish water. Adults and juveniles in these habitats hibernate in winter or aestivate in dry seasons under stones or damp logs near the pond.

Bed Bugs
Family Cimicidae

The common bed bug belongs to a small family of nocturnal, parasitic bugs that pierce the skin of warm-blooded hosts and suck a little blood.

The members of this family are flat, oval, and reddish brown. Their flatness helps them to get close to the host, to avoid being brushed off, and to hide in tight places. Their short length (less than ¼ inch, or 6 mm) also fits them for concealment. During the day they lurk in or near nests or resting places of their hosts. The common bed bug *(Cimex lectularius)* hides in crevices and holes in furniture and mattresses during the day and comes out at night to feed on sleeping people. The tiny puncture it makes can cause some skin irritation, but the bed bug has not been implicated as a disease carrier.

The female common bed bug lays from 50 to 200 whitish eggs in cracks and fissures in furniture, walls, floors, or debris in unhygienic homes and hotels. When the young hatch, they are shaped like the adult but are pale-colored and red-eyed. After five molts, they reach maturity. From egg to adult takes seven weeks in warm climates and up to six months in cold ones.

Plant Bugs
Family Miridae

This is a huge group of common small insects that feed primarily on plants, though a few suck the juices from insect eggs, aphids, and other insects. Each kind of herbivore is usually limited to one or a few specific host plants, although the tarnished plant bug, a widespread northern hemisphere pest, is an exception and feeds on several kinds. It and the cotton fleahopper are among the worst of many species that severely afflict commercial crops, both by damaging foliage and by transmitting plant diseases.

Internal plant tissues of living or dead plants serve as the hidden oviposition site for plant-bug eggs, the egg being the overwintering stage except for a few species that hibernate as adults. Most plant bugs have only one generation a year.

Mirid bugs are small, slender, soft, and variously, often gaily, colored. Some are excellent mimics of ants.

▲ Tarnished Plant Bug on thistle
Mirid on grass ▶

▲ Nymph ▼ Adult Assassin Bug

Assassin Bugs
Family Reduviidae

About 2,500 species of assassin bugs roam the earth, capturing and sucking the juices of other insects and sometimes biting humans and other mammals.

Most assassin bugs hunt for their prey on the ground, under rocks and other objects, or on plants. Their eggs are laid on plants either singly or in clusters. Some young reduviids camouflage themselves by accumulating bits of debris, fluff, or leaf particles on their sticky body surfaces.

Assassin bugs are medium-to-large insects of dark hue, sometimes with touches of red or orange. The pointed head is elongate, with a long "neck" to the rear of the small, protruding eyes.

The "masked hunter," one kind of assassin bug, feeds on engorged bed bugs, and in the process of searching for them in habitations occasionally bites people. A group of American assassin bugs are called "kissing bugs" because they bite the faces of sleeping people. While piercing human skin, a South American assassin bug can transmit the trypanosome parasites that cause Chagas' disease.

Lace Bugs
Family Tingidae

Take an unremarkable, small bug and glue on top of it some delicate, starched lace extending beyond the body all around, and you will have one of the most beautiful kinds of insects, a lace bug. The "lace" on an adult lace bug is not perforated: it is merely a textural pattern of narrow ridges surrounding depressed areas. Of course, the bug would have to be admired under a microscope, for these insects are less than 1/5 inch (5 mm) long.

Lace bugs live in unorganized colonies on the undersides of leaves and suck plant juices. When abundant, they become serious pests of trees, ornamental and other shrubs, and crops. Occasionally, they can be used to suppress unwanted plants, as in the case of a Mexican species imported into Hawaii to control lantana.

Lace-bug eggs are laid on or in plants. The young—dark and spiny or smooth and scale-like—do not resemble the delicate, pale adults but have similar feeding habits.

Some 700 species of lace bugs are distributed throughout most regions of the world, with most in the northern hemisphere.

Stink Bugs or Shield Bugs
Family Pentatomidae

These robust bugs are not the only ones with scent glands, but they are common and conspicuous and so have acquired the label "stink bug." When a stink bug is attacked by a predator, the scent glands emit a disagreeable odor as one means of defense. The alternate name of these bugs derives from their shield-like, roughly triangular, outline.

Stink bugs are heavy-bodied insects of medium-to-large size ($1/5$ to $1½$ inches or 5-40 mm in length). Eyes, wings, and legs are well developed. The coloring is often quiet (green, brown, or black) in temperate climates, although there are many exceptions, such as the spectacular harlequin bug, a crop pest with red, black, white, and yellow markings. In the tropics their gorgeous coloring and grotesque shapes make the stink bugs among the more remarkable insects.

Some stink bugs suck plant juices, some insect juices, and some will attack plants only if their preferred insect food is unavailable. Many members of this large family—more than 5,000 species—are agricultural pests, and in the tropics they are also known to transmit fungus diseases of plants.

Periodical Cicadas
Family Cicadidae

Among the world's longest lived insects are the periodical cicadas (often incorrectly called "locusts"), which live only in the eastern United States. There are three species of 17-year cicadas, which live in the north and east of the region, and three species of 13-year cicadas, which occupy the more southern and western portions. The six closely resemble each other, but each has a distinctive assembling song, which is produced by both sexes.

With the ovipositor, the eggs are thrust into living twigs and hatch in about a month. The nymphs drop to the ground and burrow down to deep roots, into which they insert their beaks to suck sap. They remain there, molting and slowly growing, for the long juvenile life. At the end of the nymphal stage, they emerge from the ground as winged adults.

From eggs laid in a given place, hordes of adults of the same species will emerge exactly 17 (or 13) years later, enabling experts to predict confidently when the next mass emergence will occur in a given area.

▲ Cicada nymph
17-Year Cicada ▶

Treehoppers
Family Membracidae

Among the most amusing insects in appearance are the small treehoppers, with their wildly exotic shapes. The crest of the thorax, extending forward over the head and backward over the abdomen, is humped, spined, or ridged and often ornamented with hooks, bulbs, and prongs. Each species has a characteristic shape, the tropical ones the most bizarre of all. The shapes evolved to camouflage the insects while feeding quietly on exposed plant stems that have thorns, buds, and bumps.

Treehoppers are usually less than ½ inch (13 mm) long. The head is vertically oriented. The four membranous wings are often hidden beneath the projecting thorax. With powerfully developed hindlegs, treehoppers jump as well as walk and fly. Like many related insects, they excrete honeydew (a sweet, sticky liquid), and the ants that are attracted to the honeydew benefit the treehoppers by driving off enemies.

▲ Spittlebug larva in protective froth ▲ Adult

▼ Leafhopper nymph ▲ Red-banded Leafhoppers ▼ Leafhopper on Heliconia

Spittlebugs or Froghoppers
Family Cercopidae

The cercopids are called froghoppers because some of them are frog-like, with their broad heads, squat bodies, large eyes, and hopping ability. The name "spittlebugs" is also used, because the nymphs are protected from enemies and desiccation by a large blob of whitish froth resembling spit. This froth is created by its inhabitant, by blowing air from a special abdominal duct into a liquid excreted through the anus. An additional viscous secretion from other glands keeps the froth from being dispersed by moderate rain. The nymph stays in its frothy cover attached to a plant until its final molt, after which it becomes a free-roaming adult.

Greenish or brownish, these plain-colored insects are small (usually no more than ¼ inch, or 6 mm long). The beak, four membranous wings, and the tent-like position of the wings at rest are typical features of the Homoptera, the vast suborder of Hemiptera to which the spittlebugs belong.

Spittlebugs feed on herbs, shrubs, and trees, and only a very few species ever occur in damaging numbers.

Leafhoppers
Family Cicadellidae

Extremely abundant in numbers and kinds, these tiny, colorful plant-suckers constitute the largest family in the order Hemiptera. They actively fly, jump, and run sideways. When sucking juices from plants, they weaken or kill the host and spread plant diseases. Almost all types and sizes of plants, from grasses to trees, are attacked by leafhoppers, and each species of insect prefers certain plants. Leafhopper populations are partly reduced by many predators and parasites, such as specific wasps, twisted-wing insects, and even carnivorous moth caterpillars, but serious economic damage results when they swarm on cultivated fruits and vegetable crops.

The eggs are inserted into slits made by the ovipositor in soft or hard plant tissues. When laid in autumn, the eggs overwinter, although in many species the adults or nymphs hibernate in weeds or litter. From one to six generations follow during the warm months. Leafhoppers, like aphids, produce honeydew and are therefore similarly tended by ants.

Fulgorid Planthoppers
Superfamily Fulgoroidea

One gigantic fulgorid in Brazil has an enlarged head resembling that of a crocodile. It was mistakenly believed to be luminous, so the old common name for this group was "lanternflies," although these insects do not produce light.

Fulgorids are plant-eaters but not usually agricultural pests. They are found most commonly in the tropics and subtropics, with the smaller species occurring in temperate zones. Distinctive features of these insects are the network of veins in the outer end of the hindwings and the white, waxy, tail-like filaments exuded from abdominal glands.

Fulgorids have three-segmented antennae with the middle segment large and bulbous. The rounded head is often enlarged into fantastic shapes. The four glassy or leathery wings are held over the body like a tall A-frame roof. In many species the wings are longer than the body. The giant crocodile-head fulgorid has a 6-inch (15 cm) wingspread, but other species are less than 1/8 inch (3 mm) long. The young resemble their parents in habits.

▲ Adult, Costa Rica ▼ Fulgorid nymph ▲ Adult, India

Adult and wax-covered nymph

Jumping Plantlice
Family Psyllidae

The jumping plantlice look like cicadas but are very tiny ($1/12$-$1/5$ inch or 2-5 mm). Widely distributed in temperate areas, these plant feeders often become pests of olive and other fruit trees, tomatoes, potatoes, and many other crops and ornamental plants as well as wild plants. The family is especially well represented in Australia, where they are called lerp insects and have taken over the role of aphids. Lerp insects produce honeydew, which is collected and eaten by the aborigines.

Psyllid nymphs are oval, flat, often fringed around the edges, and have large wing pads. Many exude honeydew and some also exude a waxy fluff to cover themselves. Nymphs of some species are scale-like and inactive, staying in one place on a plant.

The glassy wings of adult jumping plantlice have few veins, and the forewings are larger than the hind ones. Large, slightly protuberant eyes and long, thread-like antennae are other prominent features.

Whiteflies

Family Aleyrodidae

A white, powdery wax, exuded from glands, covers the transparent wings and body of the tiny whiteflies. Their eyes have a peculiar shape—long ovals constricted in the middle. The most familiar and common species, the greenhouse whitefly, is distributed worldwide in greenhouses and is seen occasionally on house plants. Another very abundant species is the citrus whitefly, a pest wherever citrus is grown. This large family lives on a great number of plants in temperate and tropical areas.

A newly hatched juvenile whitefly moves around easily but at the first molt loses its legs and antennae; succeeding larval stages are sedentary and scale-like, often covered with cottony wax and fringed with elaborate wax plates or filaments. Immature whiteflies produce honeydew so copiously that it frequently drips down onto leaves below. Horticultural problems arise not only from the insects' sucking plant juices but from the sooty black mold which, in warm climates, grows on the honeydew: the two substances together coat the leaf surface and thus inhibit photosynthesis.

Aphids or Plantlice
Family Aphididae

Aphids are tiny, soft-bodied plant-feeders. They typically remain motionless for long periods with proboscis inserted, pumping up liquid nutrients. Aphids seriously damage crops, not only by their feeding activities but by transmitting plant diseases. Though prolific, their numbers are restrained somewhat by lady beetles, specific parasites, and a host of other enemies. Aphids produce honeydew, a sugary liquid prized by certain ants, which tend aphids as we tend cows for milk.

These insects have complex reproductive cycles. Most species overwinter as eggs on the primary host plant. In the spring the eggs hatch and may produce only stem-mothers which, without mating, give birth to young, not eggs. These offspring, all daughters, may be winged or wingless, and the winged ones may move to the secondary host plant. Many successive all-female, usually wingless, generations commonly occur during the summer. In the autumn, winged males and usually wingless females are produced and mate, whereupon each fertilized female lays several eggs, which pass the winter.

The color yellow strongly attracts aphids, possibly because it has the wavelength of plant pigments they use in finding new hosts.

Mealybugs and Scale Insects
Superfamily Coccoidea

Mealybugs and scale insects suck the sap from any part of plants, from roots to top, and many species form galls. The 6,000 species live on a wide variety of plants, which suffer heavy damage if not protected.

Juveniles and the wingless females are protected by a fluffy or grainy waxy secretion (mealybugs) or a hard or soft hemispherical scale (scale insects). The eggs are usually laid in loose masses of wax or in sacs beneath the female. Some females bear live young.

Newly hatched juveniles have legs and crawl around in search of a permanent feeding site; but after settling and inserting the beak in the plant, they molt to a blob-like, sedentary stage in which the legs may be entirely lost. All coccoids are eyeless or have very small eyes. Males may be wingless but crawl actively; they do not feed.

Many mealybugs and scale insects are so specialized as motionless feeding machines that even expert entomologists tend not to recognize them as insects.

▼ Scale Insect on citrus ▲ Mealybugs

Scale Insects

▲ "Hellgrammite" ▼ Adult Dobsonfly

Dobsonflies and Alderflies
Order Megaloptera

In cool, fresh water live the gilled, predacious larvae called "hellgrammites," "crawlers," or "toe-biters," which are immature dobsonflies. Both the larvae and the adults form an important link in the food chain as prey of large fish.

This very small order (about 300 species) occurs mostly in temperate zones. The four gauzy wings are similar in size and shape, and have many veins, unbranched where they meet the edges of the wings. Wingspan is 6 inches (15 cm) or less. Alderflies are much smaller and darker than dobsonflies. At rest the wings are held roof-like or nearly flat on the back. Megaloptera have soft, flexible bodies and bulging eyes. In some species the huge mouthparts of the male are sickle-shaped and nearly half the length of the body, but adult dobsonflies are not known to feed.

The eggs are laid in cake-like masses on shrubs or objects near water. Pupation takes place in a simple cell under rocks at the stream edge, and the whole life cycle—most of it spent in the larval stage—lasts from one to three years in different species.

Lacewings and Antlions
Order Neuroptera

Many of the insects in this small order are beautifully colored and patterned. All have four similar glassy wings that are held roof-like over the back when at rest. Characteristically, the network of veins in the wings is complex, with numerous crossveins in the center and forked branches along the margins. Large eyes and chewing mouthparts occupy most of the head.

Neuropterans have an abrupt (four-stage) life cycle. The larvae are predacious and terrestrial except in one minor family whose aquatic larvae feed on freshwater sponges. All larvae have thoracic but not abdominal legs and huge sickle-shaped jaws, with the main parts held tightly together around a hollow inner space through which the prey's juices are sucked. The larvae lack a continuous gut, so feces are stored in the body until later life.

The pupa lies in a curved position inside a silk cocoon, and when mature cuts its way out with its mouthparts before the adult emerges. Certain Neuroptera have scent glands that may produce either a citronella type of odor or a musky one.

Like the related snakeflies and dobsonflies, these are ancient, conservative insects and are well known from early in the fossil record.

Green Lacewings
Family Chrysopidae

The name Chrysopidae comes from the Greek for "golden eye," for the eyes of these attractive and fragile insects have a brilliant golden luster. The delicate wings with their fine network of veins suggested the popular name of lacewings. Wingspan ranges from ⅓ to 2½ inches (8-65 mm). The antennae are very long and thread-like. Adult lacewings are most active in the twilight or at night and often come to lights.

The eggs of almost all species are laid singly at the top of a very long stalk attached to a leaf. The voracious larvae ("aphid lions") seek soft-bodied, slow-moving prey. A shield of debris (often the sucked-out shells of their prey) is borne on the backs of some species. To pupate, the larva seeks a sheltered spot under loose bark or a leaf and spins silk from an anal spinneret into a round, woolly cocoon. Some species spend more than one winter in the cocoon.

Since both larvae and adults destroy huge numbers of pest insects, the lacewings are considered highly beneficial.

◀ Adult Antlion, Spain

Antlions
Family Myrmeleontidae

Antlions or "doodlebugs" are the plump, hairy larvae that lie in ambush at the bottom of funnel-shaped pits in dry, dusty soil. Each pit is dug by one occupant, using the long jaws as shovels to throw the sand up and out. The trap may be up to an inch (25 mm) deep. The antlion lies buried with its head protruding at the bottom of the funnel. When an unwary ant or other insect tumbles over the edge of the sliding sand pit, the antlion seizes it. These fierce creatures are able to move quickly backward through the sand. The pits are often clustered under the overhanging edges of rocks, stumps, or isolated buildings, especially in areas where rain is frequent. Not all species construct pits: some just lie in wait under objects or debris.

Antlion eggs are laid singly in dry soil or sand. The larva pupates in the sand within a globular cocoon. When the pupa is mature, it works its way up to the surface while still in the pupal skin before emerging as an adult.

Adult antlions look somewhat like damselflies but have prominent, slightly clubbed antennae, and much softer bodies.

▲ Adult Antlion ▼ "Doodlebug"

Snakeflies
Order Raphidiodea

Confined to the northern hemisphere except for one Chilean species the hundred species of snakeflies occur widely in Europe and Asia but in North America are found only from the Rocky Mountains westward.

These small- to medium-sized insects earned their name because the front part of the thorax and often the head are very long and narrow, resembling the raised front end of an aroused snake. Except for that feature, they generally look like relatives of the lacewings.

The predacious adults feed on small, weak insects because their legs are not specialized for seizing prey. They are reddish and sit on tree trunks, foliage, or flowers. The female's long, slender ovipositor enables it to thrust eggs into crevices in the bark.

The immature stages are passed under the loose bark of conifers, eucalyptus, and other trees or under needle litter beneath pines, and so snakefly distribution coincides with that of the trees. The larvae feed on small insects. The pupae do not feed but are active and mobile.

Scorpionflies
Order Mecoptera

The scorpionflies got their name because the male genitalia in more than half of the 400 species are enlarged into a bulb that is held curved over the back and vaguely resembles a scorpion's stinger (but is harmless). A more characteristic feature is the peculiar vertical lengthening of the face, somewhat like that of a baby elephant.

Scorpionflies have four wings, long and simple antennae, and slender legs. Some look like crane flies except for having four, instead of two, wings. Body length is mostly from ½ to 1 inch (12-25 mm). The wings are often handsomely spotted (a few are wingless) and the body color dull. They are slow fliers and like cool, damp woods.

Adult scorpionflies are omnivorous. The ones that look like crane flies spend much time hanging by the front legs from foliage, capturing prey with the grasping hindlegs. An Australian species also mates while suspended, after enticing the female to him with food held in his mouth. Another kind of courtship is shown by the typical scorpionflies: the male spits on a leaf and while the female feeds on the hardened saliva he mates with her.

Cat Flea

Fleas
Order Siphonaptera

The 1,400 species of fleas pierce the skin, inject saliva, and suck the blood of a wide variety of mammals and a few birds. Most kinds of fleas attack only one specific host but others may take blood from several. Dog and cat fleas prefer dogs and cats but, rarely, will bite other mammals. The oriental rat flea, which also sucks human blood, is the vector of the dreaded bubonic plague.

Fleas are wingless. Their long hindlegs enable them to jump astounding distances. For slipping through hair or feathers, fleas are extremely flattened laterally, have short forelegs, claws, and comb-like bristles.

Adult fleas can survive as long as a year without feeding. Usually they do not remain on the host continuously, but live in the host's nest, in dry soil, or in cracks and under rugs in houses. A blood-meal is necessary for female reproduction. The eggs are laid in the host's habitat or sometimes on the host (but soon fall off). The worm-like larvae feed on debris, and when mature spin a silk-and-earth cocoon. The complete metamorphosis takes from a month to more than a year.

Two-winged Flies
Order Diptera

The true flies have only two wings (the front pair). The wings are membranous and transparent, rarely having hairs or scales. The former hindwings have become reduced to minute clubs (halteres). These vibrate during flight and act as gyroscopic sense organs that inform the flying insect when it starts to roll, pitch, or yaw and enable it to regulate its turns. Flies have large compound eyes, sometimes covering most of the head. The antennae take many forms, including those that are filamentous, or like long strings of beads, and others that have only a few oddly shaped segments.

This is one of the largest and most successful orders of insects. Estimations of the numbers of species, both known and undiscovered, go as high as 150,000.

Diptera undergo abrupt metamorphosis, with a non-feeding pupal stage between larva and adult. The legless larvae feed in moist places—water, soil, rotting organic material—or on plant or animal tissues. The pupae of most flies have no cocoon, and many pupate inside the last larval skin.

Tachina Fly

House Fly

Midge

Crane Flies
Family Tipulidae

This immense family is the largest in the order. Crane flies are long-legged and narrow-winged, with slender bodies and usually thread-like antennae. Some have spotted or clouded wings. The delicate legs are easily broken off (it is common to see crane flies with fewer than six legs) and are useless for running. They are used to land and to cling to objects when the fly is resting. The head is partly retracted into the thorax. The tiniest crane flies are only ¼ inch (6 mm) in wingspan and the largest about 3 inches (75 mm).

Crane flies love moisture: the larvae are aquatic or live in wet soil or rotting vegetation, and the adults abound in damp woods and near streams. Most larvae (tough-skinned "leather-jackets") feed on leaf mold but a few damage the roots or even leaves of living plants. Little is known of the adults' feeding habits but some may drink nectar. They are not predacious and do not bite mammals.

"Daddy-longlegs" is a name sometimes applied to crane flies but, unlike the arachnids of that name, the flies have wings (usually), only six legs, and a distinct head with antennae.

Mosquitoes
Family Culicidae

Most female mosquitoes must have a blood-meal to mature their eggs. Various species have different blood hosts: mammals, birds, reptiles, amphibians, or even surface-dwelling fish. Male mosquitoes drink only nectar or water—it is only the females that bite. Large courtship swarms of males may form near emergence sites of virgin females. The pitch of the wing hum is used in sexual recognition.

The eggs are deposited singly or in rafts in every imaginable watery site: from tide pools to discarded containers to tree holes. Each species of mosquito has a preferred habitat for its eggs and larvae.

The aquatic larvae ("wrigglers") rest just under the surface film, inhale through breathing tubes at the tail ends of their bodies, and feed on microorganisms. The pupae are also aquatic.

Certain mosquitoes are the carriers of dreaded diseases such as malaria, yellow fever, dengue fever, and elephantiasis. For some of these they are simply mechanical carriers, while for others they are intermediate hosts for the disease organisms, which complete their development in the animals bitten by the mosquitoes.

Midge pupa

Midges
Family Chironomidae

The fragile, mosquito-like midges are noted for their male courtship swarms, which rise and fall in the air on summer evenings near water. Individual females fly into the swarm, find a mate, and the coupled pair disappears into the vegetation. The males die within a few days, but the females live longer to mature and lay their eggs. These midges never bite or feed as adults. They may come to lights in great numbers.

Midges lay their eggs in strings and masses in the water. Worm-like larvae make tubes in the mud and feed by filtering plankton from a stream of water passing through the tube. "Bloodworms" are those that have a red oxygen-bearing substance in their blood.

Each species of midge larva can be found in its own kind of water: still or swift, stagnant or fresh, saline, or of various temperatures. Warmer water permits faster development and more generations per year. These larvae are a major food of small fish and aquatic insects.

◀ Mosquito larva

▲ Biting Midge sucking on Walkingstick ▼ Black Fly, Brazil

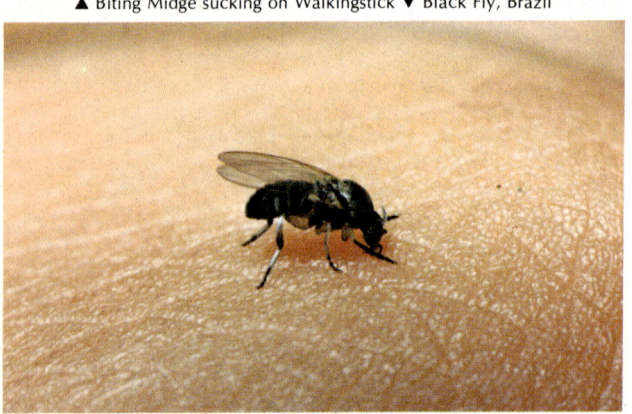

Biting Midges
Family Ceratopogonidae

These tiny flies are commonly called "no-see-ums" or "punkies." In spite of their speck-like size they bite ferociously and attack in swarms. Certain groups prey on warm-blooded vertebrates or on frogs, but the main targets of some are other insects. The latter kind delicately suck blood from wing veins of moths, lacewings, and dragonflies, and cling tenaciously while the victims fly. Even engorged female mosquitoes may be robbed of their blood-meal.

Most of the larvae are aquatic. Not much is known about their food habits; they are probably scavengers.

Near marshes, lakes, and ocean beaches in cool northern regions the biting midges are a special nuisance to people and seem to be most active in early morning, dusk, or on humid days. A very few species transmit parasitic worms to warm-blooded animals. On the credit side, some females effectively pollinate flowers: the cocoa plant is said to be dependent on them for this service.

Black Flies
Family Simuliidae

The hump-backed black flies are familiar pests to hunters, anglers, and hikers. They are also called "buffalo gnats" or "turkey gnats." Unlike midges, black flies have stout bodies and short, broad wings.

Female black flies suck the blood of warm-blooded animals during daylight hours. Clouds of them attack at once, so loss of blood can be serious, possibly even fatal, to sedentary grazing animals or ground-feeding fowl, especially since black flies occasionally transmit diseases and internal parasites.

Simuliids are abundant near water although the adults roam farther than most flies. The eggs are laid on the surface of water, on aquatic plants, or on wet rocks. The larvae can live only in tumbling, well-aerated streams, and must anchor themselves to rocks or plants. They filter food particles from the water and do not need to surface for air. When mature they pupate underwater.

Gall Midges
Family Cecidomyiidae

Among the fragile, minute flies in this family is the notorious Hessian fly, the most destructive wheat insect. It originated in Asia, spread to Europe, and arrived in North America with the Hessian soldiers during the Revolution. With two or three generations a year, these flies proliferate and bore into the wheat stems to feed. When winter comes, the larvae hibernate.

The majority of the brightly colored gall midge larvae eat plants, often living in galls or other plant deformities caused by themselves or other insects. A number are pests of cultivated plants such as alfalfa, rice, and fruits. Pupation takes place in the plants.

The long antennae of males are festooned with loops and whorls of hairs. Both sexes have hairs and sometimes spots on the broad wings.

Horse Flies and Deer Flies
Family Tabanidae

Large and robust, the tabanids often have gorgeously colored eyes banded in iridescent colors. The eyes cover most of the head, frequently touching at the top in males. Somber in color, the body may reach a length of more than an inch (30 mm).

Male horse and deer flies eat only nectar. Females feed by cutting the flesh and sucking the oozing blood of humans, hoofed and other mammals, reptiles, and amphibians. Sometimes they transmit internal parasites and diseases such as tularemia and anthrax.

The strong-flying adults are usually found near water, for the eggs are laid on foliage overhanging streams and ponds so that the semi-aquatic larvae drop into the water after hatching. Some larvae prey on snails, insects, and other organisms, but the food habits of many are unknown. They pupate in moist leaf litter above water line. One generation a year is the norm, and the adults live for a few weeks.

Horse Fly

▲ Hessian fly ▼ Deer Fly

Robber Flies
Family Asilidae

Robber flies are superbly equipped for their trade—the capturing of live insects on the wing. They have huge, bulging eyes, grasping legs, and piercing and sucking mouthparts. To ensnare the prey the first two pairs of legs hang down, with their long bristles overlapping. The hindlegs fold and clamp the victim. Dense bristly cushions, especially on the head, protect the fly from stings and bites of the struggling victim.

The basic shape of robber flies includes a stout, humped thorax and a long, pointed abdomen, but a number of species marvelously mimic the shape and color of bees, bumble bees, and wasps.

Robber flies dwell mostly in open, forested areas or meadows. Their eggs are laid in the soil or on bark or plants. The majority of the larvae are vegetarians and live in the soil.

Bee Flies
Family Bombyliidae

About half the members of this family look and behave like wild bees. Dark, stout, and hairy, they hover over flowers sucking nectar with the long, stiff proboscis. They even make a buzzing sound when captured. But unlike bees, the wings are outstretched to the sides when at rest. A few large species look and act like long-legged wasps.

The other half of the family is brightly patterned with scale-like hairs and has a short proboscis. Their food is not known (possibly nectar, honeydew, and liquids from rotting flesh).

Many bee-fly larvae live in the underground nests of solitary bees and feed on their young. Some are internal parasites of other insects.

Sunny, dry, scrub country is the favored habitat of bee flies. The rather short-lived adults begin to appear in spring.

Dance Flies
Family Empididae

Some dance-fly courtship is a fascinating example of what seems at first glance to be gallantry: the male presents to the female an insect, often enclosed in a silken ball or a frothy balloon. This is not a gift but probably a diversion to keep the female occupied so she won't seize and eat the male. The offering also stimulates sexual response in the females of some advanced species.

Courtship in many dance flies takes place during the swarming, aerial "dances" that are typically seen moving up and down above the surface of water on warm summer evenings.

Dance flies are predators of other insects and look like robber flies but are smaller. Most common in temperate zones, dance flies like coolness and moisture. Their larvae live in moist places near water, under sand, mud, seaweed heaps, moss, or rotting wood. Only one small group has become completely aquatic. The larvae are primarily carnivorous, feeding on live or dead insects. This is a very large and still little-known family.

Long-legged Flies
Family Dolichopodidae

Much smaller than a house fly, the typical long-legged fly has brilliantly colored eyes covering most of its head and the body is a vivid, metallic green or blue. The legs of some males are ornamented with bright tufts of hairs or the wings are conspicuously marked, and these are waved in front of the female during courtship.

Abundant on foliage in daylight, the beautiful dolichopodids hunt on foot. The front pair of legs is the longest and causes the forepart of the body to stand higher than the back end. A section of the mouthparts is developed into an extended, spongy bag to engulf the prey while its skin is being torn by hard mouthparts. The bag gives a long, vertical look to the head of the fly.

In appearance, diet, and habitat, the larvae of the long-legged flies resemble those of the dance flies; the pupae are enclosed in cocoons of silk or of sand and mud glued together with gelatinous secretions.

Flower Flies
Family Syrphidae

Second only to bees as valuable pollinators of flowers, the flower flies live solely on nectar and honeydew and often have elongated mouthparts enabling them to reach the sweet liquid in deep flowers.

Different species of flower flies are exact matches for specific kinds of bees, bumble bees, or wasps. The bee mimics are broad-waisted and fuzzy; the wasp mimics narrow-waisted and smooth. Color patterns amazingly enhance the mimicry. Some mimics live in the nests of their models and the adults flying together are almost indistinguishable.

The scavenging maggots of flower flies live in ant, bee, or termite nests or in dung, rotting materials, boggy soil, or shallow water. Gardeners may find them in stored or buried flower bulbs. The aquatic ones have retractable snorkel tubes through which they inhale air from the surface, and some also have gills.

Fruit Flies
Family Tephritidae

Among the many commercially important fruit pests in this family is the famous Mediterranean fruit fly ("Medfly"), which inhabits warm regions all over the world. Its eggs are inserted into cracks in the skin of oranges and other fruits and the larvae feed inside. Eventually the fruit falls and the maggots emerge to pupate in the soil.

Fruit flies are tiny, slightly bristly, and usually have elaborately mottled wing patterns. The large head is set on a very narrow "neck." Short antennae are flanked by big, often iridescent green eyes.

The larvae of different species of fruit flies prefer particular kinds of plants and specific parts of each plant. Some are miners, gall-makers, or borers. Flies that attack thistles, burrs, and weeds are often purposely imported into some areas to control such plants.

Vinegar Flies
Family Drosophilidae

Probably the most studied insects in the world are the species of *Drosophila*. Hundreds of biologists around the world use them for experiments in heredity and evolution, and students in colleges and schools rear them to learn genetic principles. These small flies are especially useful because their salivary gland chromosomes are giant-sized and easily examined under microscopes.

Drosophila are popularly called "fruit flies" because they are often found around decaying fruit and garbage, but it is fermenting juice that attracts them, not just in fruit but in leaf mold, sap, honeydew, milk, and other non-meat substances. The fly larvae feed on yeasts that cause the fermentation. Other kinds of drosophilid larvae scavenge in bee nests, mine leaves, or prey on small insects. One species, an internal parasite of scale insects, was imported from Australia into California to control a citrus scale. Their greatest diversity has developed in Hawaii.

House Flies and Stable Flies
Family Muscidae

All over the world the common house fly *(Musca domestica)* is associated with people. It does not bite but mops up organic liquids of all kinds, contaminates food and thereby may spread diseases. It develops incredibly fast (a week or two in the tropics) and may have ten generations a year even in temperate climates. In fall the house flies move into buildings to hibernate. The larvae live in any kind of decaying plant or animal matter, especially dung. Where the automobile has replaced the horse, a prime breeding site (horse manure) has been eliminated.

If an insect resembling a house fly bites, it is probably the stable fly, a species that attacks humans and domestic animals and breeds in horse manure. Other biters (both sexes) are the horn and face flies of cattle.

Most muscids feed and develop in decaying organic matter but some larvae are predators or plant-feeders.

House Fly: ▼ Puparium and larvae ▲ Adult ▼ Adult blowing bubble

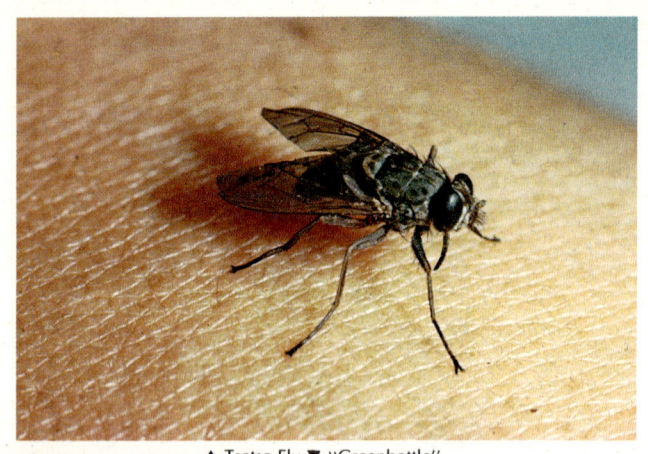

▲ Tsetse Fly ▼ "Greenbottle"

Tsetse Flies
Family Glossinidae

In the "fly belts" of Africa the tsetse flies are greatly feared. Some of the 22 species are the carriers of human sleeping sickness and of certain other diseases fatal to cattle, horses, and camels. Both sexes of tsetses are daylight biters. As they feed on the blood of wild mammals, especially antelopes, they ingest the disease-causing protozoans. Immunity to the diseases has evolved in the wild game but when a fly transmits the infection to domestic animals or people, serious symptoms develop. Each species of tsetse fly tends to bite one type of host, but the two most dangerous to man bite many mammals and even reptiles.

This family is distantly related to that of the house fly, one distinction being that tsetses lay larvae, not eggs. One egg at a time hatches inside the female and the larva grows to full size there, fed like a human fetus on nutrients from the mother. At least three blood-meals are required by a mother while carrying one larva. When the larva is deposited on loose, moist soil, it tunnels in and pupates there. About a dozen larvae are produced by one female—an amazingly small fecundity for an insect.

Blow Flies
Family Calliphoridae

"Bluebottles" and "greenbottles" are other names for blow flies. They are shaped like house flies but have a metallic sheen on their bright, green or blue bodies. Primarily carrion-feeders, the maggots in a mass are an unpleasant sight to many people but these larvae are valuable agents in disposing of animal carcasses. Some blow-fly larvae, such as the screw worm, feed around wounds or in the nostrils of live animals and become a serious veterinary problem in sheep and cattle.

Noisily buzzing, blow flies come into houses frequently but are less dangerous than house flies as disease carriers because they are not so attracted to human food.

Laid on newly dead animals, the eggs must have high humidity to hatch. The larvae excrete ammonia and digestive enzymes to partly dissolve the meat before they start feeding. For pupation they leave the carcass and seek a dry, sheltered site. A few members of this family have become blood-suckers or parasites.

Flesh Flies
Family Sarcophagidae

Adult flesh flies are large and bristly with checkered gray bodies. They resemble blow flies except for their non-metallic coloring. The adults do not bite; they feed only on honeydew, nectar, and other plant liquids.

The eggs hatch inside the female and the young larvae are deposited on suitable feeding sites—most are parasites of invertebrate animals and destroy countless numbers of insects. Their hosts are snails, spiders and their eggs, grasshoppers, beetles, and the like. Some larvae live in bee, wasp, or termite nests, and a few feed on the flesh of vertebrates and may cause severe injury to domestic animals but rarely to humans. Many eat only decaying materials. The larvae develop rapidly, and in warm places they have several generations a year.

Tachina Flies
Family Tachinidae

The larvae of tachina flies are wholly parasitic in the adults and larvae of insects and of other arthropods. They destroy huge numbers of insects, especially caterpillars, and therefore are highly beneficial from a human standpoint. Some species of these flies feed only on one specific host while others are not particular. The eggs are usually deposited on the body of the host and the larvae burrow in and feed internally, but some tachina flies lay vast numbers of minute eggs on foliage and the eggs are ingested along with the leaf by a host insect and hatch in the gut. Alternatively, the eggs may hatch while on the leaf and the larvae must then attach themselves to a passing host. Pupation occurs within the host or in the ground.

This second largest family of Diptera is composed of very bristly, medium-sized flies; a few are mimics of bees or wasps, but most look like spiny house flies.

Rabbit Bot Fly

Bot and Warble Flies
Family Oestridae

Bot-fly larvae live in the nasal and sinus cavities of wild and domesticated hoofed animals. They feed on mucus and stimulate its production by scraping the tissues, causing inflammation and congestion in the host. About ten months is spent in the larval stage. When mature the larvae are expelled and then pupate in the ground.

Warble flies parasitize cattle and other hoofed mammals. The eggs are laid on the host animal, especially on the legs, and the tiny new larvae burrow into the tissues. They don't remain in one area but migrate through the body for months. At last one (or more) comes to rest under the hide on the host's back, where it produces a "warble" or swelling, punctured with a tiny hole through which the larva gets air. When mature the larva leaves the warble and pupates in the ground.

Adult oestrid flies are large, hairy, and brightly patterned, somewhat resembling small bumble bees.

Caddisflies
Order Trichoptera

All caddisflies have aquatic larvae, most of which construct portable houses, or cases, of various materials—stones, sand, snail shells, twigs, or conifer needles—bound with silk. Only the head, thorax, and legs protrude from the case. These larvae can be found on stream bottoms or submerged plants in fresh, flowing water, where they derive nourishment from water plants or minute organisms. As a major source of food for freshwater fish they are important in the food chain.

Strings or masses of eggs are laid in or near the water. Most of the life cycle (ordinarily one generation a year) is spent in the larval stage. Pupation occurs in the larval case or in a jelly-like cocoon. This is the only order of insects in which all species pupate underwater.

Caddisflies resemble small, drab, hairy moths but have weak chewing mouthparts, with which they lick up nectar. During the day the adults hide in cool, damp places, often near water, becoming active at dusk. They are preyed on by bats, frogs, birds, and many insects, and most survive only a few days.

▲ Adult Caddisfly ▼ Caddis Worm feeding on scum underwater

Moths and Butterflies
Order Lepidoptera

The gorgeous colors and patterns lavishly displayed on the wings of many butterflies and moths have an adaptive purpose, such as sexual recognition (species recognizing their own kind), concealment, absorbing solar heat, and signals to predators (mainly birds) of disagreeable taste.

The 112,000 species of butterflies and moths have a dense covering of minute, overlapping scales on wings and body, and most have a flexible sucking proboscis that coils up like a watch spring when not in use. They have large compound eyes and two pairs of wings.

The vast majority of Lepidoptera are moths. Some moths are dayfliers, like all butterflies. Butterflies differ from nearly all moths in having a knob at the tip of each antenna.

The life cycle takes from a few weeks to two years in most species. Hibernation may occur at any stage. The eggs are laid in any season except the coldest; females find the right food plant to lay on by sensing certain leaf chemicals through chemoreceptors in their front feet.

Female Ghost Moth

Ghost Moths and Swifts
Family Hepialidae

The ghost moths are only dimly visible as they flicker eerily through the dusk. The swifts are noted for rapid flight. Robust, hairy, and medium to very large in size, the hepialid moths reach their peak in Australia. Many have beautiful silvery markings and some are brilliant-green. The pale, wrinkled caterpillars of large Australian hepialids, called "wichity grubs," are a favorite food of native peoples in the desert.

Some hepialid caterpillars bore vertically into the trunks of living trees and shrubs and eat the regenerating plant tissue around the tunnel entrance. When ready to pupate, they seal the tunnels with silken wads and retire to the deepest part. Other larvae feed on roots and some are severe range pests in the southern hemisphere.

Courtship among the ghost moths is almost unique among the Lepidoptera in having reversed sex roles: the females search for and court the males.

◀ Swallowtail Butterfly

Tineid on carpet

Clothes Moths and Their Allies
Family Tineidae

Only a few members of this family attack clothes. The majority live outdoors, where their larvae feed on dry organic matter and fungi. Some live in ant nests, some web together leaves or feed under bark, others tunnel in fungi. Dried grain is the food of certain ones that infest buildings.

The tineids are tiny, drab moths with erect, bristly scales and hairs on their heads and antennae.

The several species of clothes moths have special wool-digesting enzymes and are among the very few animals that can get nourishment from wool. The three main species of clothes moths originated in the Old World but are now worldwide. The commonest is the webbing clothes moth; when ready to pupate its larva makes a cocoon out of particles of its food (wool, fur, feathers, and other animal products). The larva of the case-making clothes moth feeds on the same materials but makes a parchment-like case that is open on both ends. The larva of the third species, the tapestry or carpet moth, tunnels through masses of wool materials.

Bagworm larva

Bagworm Moths
Family Psychidae

Most female bagworms never develop wings and many never leave their larval homes—cases or bags of twigs, leaves, or bark cemented together with silk. These may be as much as 5 inches (12.5 cm) long but are usually much smaller. The bag is open at both ends; from the front end the larva's head and thorax stick out, and from the other end excrement is expelled.

Protected by the case, the caterpillar moves about and feeds. When ready to pupate in the autumn, it attaches the front end of the case to a tree or shrub and closes both ends. Following pupation the female of most species does not leave the bag, but mates and lays eggs within it. As many as 3,000 eggs are laid by a single female of certain species. The caterpillar of a male bagworm also makes a case and pupates in it, but at maturity the pupa pushes partly out, and the winged adult emerges and flies away.

Bagworms live in woods and shrubbery and even grass. The larvae feed on foliage, including that of conifers, lichens, and mosses. The adults do not feed.

Clearwing Moths
Family Aegeriidae

The clearwings don't look like moths. All are mimics of wasps, with large, clear (scaleless) areas in the wings, vividly contrasting colors, and wasp-like behavior. Slender bodies, long legs, and smooth surfaces further enhance the image, but none of them has the narrow wasp-waist. They are dark, frequently metallic-looking and marked with yellow or red. These small, diurnal moths hover over flowers and fly swiftly.

As borers in trunks, bark, or roots, caterpillars of many of the clearwings severely damage cultivated plants and trees. Some feed on plants from within galls made by themselves or other insects. The mobile, spiny pupae transform within the larval burrows.

One very serious pest in this family is the peachtree borer, whose caterpillars bore into the trunk just below ground level, feed on the roots, and overwinter there.

Pink Bollworm larvae

Gelechiid Moths
Family Gelechiidae

The pink bollworm (a pest of cotton plants) and the Angoumois grain moth (which infests stored grain) are two of the important worldwide species in this family of tiny moths. The larvae of the bollworm tunnel into the developing cotton bolls, eat the seeds, and destroy the crop. The grain moth larvae bore into the kernels of wheat, corn, and other grains and can be ruinous if uncontrolled. Infestations can be recognized by a small hole in the kernel where the adult moth has emerged.

The goldenrod gall moths are also an interesting group. They make the familiar, spindle-shaped stem gall in goldenrod and related plants. The eggs overwinter on the food plant and hatch in the spring. Later, before pupating in the gall, the larva cuts a hole, not quite through, in the upper end of the gall so that the adult moth can escape when it emerges. Often only wasp parasites escape!

Gelechiid caterpillars are all concealed feeders. Many are miners in conifer needles, leaves, fruit, or stems of plants; or they tie leaves together with silk threads to make shelters.

▲ Codling Moth ▼ Spruce Budworm larva with Wasp parasite

Codling Moth
Family Tortricidae

The codling moth, a worldwide insect pest, is of special concern because it diminishes the world's food supply. The codling moth larvae destroy vast numbers of apples, pears, walnuts, and other orchard crops. The familiar pale-bodied, dark-headed "worm" in an unsprayed apple is this species.

The subtly colored moths are about ⅝ to ⅞ inches (15-22 mm) in wing expanse. The female lays her eggs singly on the fruit and foliage of the host tree. Each year two to four generations are produced, with the life cycle lasting about 50 days. Like many tortricids, caterpillars that mature in the fall hibernate in cocoons before pupating in the spring. They spin white, felt-like cocoons under loose bark or in tree crevices, leaf litter, and similar shelters.

Tortricid moths are small, mostly nocturnal insects with forewings rather square at the outer ends. Their larvae, commonly called leafrollers, have vastly diverse behavior and foods. Those that feed on foliage roll the leaves or needles into a hideaway tied together with threads. Others resemble the codling moth by living concealed in fruit, nuts, or flower clusters.

Spruce Budworm
Family Tortricidae

One of the most destructive insects in coniferous forests is the North American spruce budworm. Its caterpillars may kill thousands of acres of spruce and balsam fir in northern areas during periodic outbreaks. The outbreaks eventually collapse, like all insect plagues, due to a combination of natural factors such as predators, parasites, diseases, adverse weather, or shortage of the right food.

The pale-green eggs of spruce budworm moths are laid in clusters on tree needles in the summer and hatch in less than two weeks. The young larvae crawl under bark scales, spin cocoon-like shelters, and overwinter. In the spring they emerge to feed on the old needles and needle-buds. When the new needles lengthen, the caterpillars tie the tips of several twigs together with silk and continue feeding on both needles and soft bark. When mature, the larvae spin a loose silk web in the nest or attached to a twig and transform into pupae. Adults fly in July.

The mottled gray or tan adult moth has a wingspan of about 1 inch (25 mm). There are very closely related pest species, especially those on jack and red pines in eastern Canada and on Douglas fir in the west.

European corn borer

Pyralid Moths
Family Pyralidae

The European corn borer is no longer confined to Europe but is widespread. It feeds in the stalks of corn (maize), sorghum, millet, hemp, dahlias, and other plants, and is among the many destructive members of this huge family.

Pyralid caterpillars have a variety of food preferences, from flowers, fruit, and leaves, to dead organic matter and live insects. The Indian meal moth spoils stored grain, nuts, and dried fruit by eating and spinning webs in them. The larvae of the greater wax moth tunnel in the wax of bee hives and soil the honey. Some pyralid caterpillars are aquatic and feed on water plants. A highly beneficial species is the Argentinian cactus moth, which was successfully introduced into Australia to control the rampant prickly-pear cactus.

Pyralid moths are small and delicate and appear to have a snout. The wings are fringed and, in most species, quietly colored.

Plume Moths
Family Pterophoridae

The wings of plume moths are deeply cleft into several divisions, like the primary wing feathers of hawks. The front wing has two, three, or four lobes or plumes; the back wing three.

Plume moths are weak fliers. When resting, they look like tiny, old-fashioned airplanes, with the wings closely rolled and stretched out at right angles to the body. These small moths are slender and pale gray, white, or brown and have legs that are spindly and long.

The newly hatched caterpillars may feed at first as leaf miners, then, as they grow, switch to exposed feeding on leaves or leaf rolling or stem boring. They rarely do serious damage to crops. The caterpillars of the grape plume moth infest vineyards and fasten the tips of leaves together with silk to conceal themselves while feeding. Plume-moth larvae pupate in the larval tunnels or attached to a plant by the tail end, usually without a cocoon.

Geometrid Moths
Family Geometridae

Geometrid caterpillars are the familiar inchworms (also called "measuringworms," "spanworms," or "loopers"). Their amusing method of locomotion is necessary because they have no middle legs on the abdomen. They can move faster than other larvae. The inchworm stretches forward and grips the substrate with its front legs, then brings the back end up near the front, causing the body to arch upward.

Geometrid larvae and adults are noted for their amazingly precise, protective resemblance to their backgrounds. Twig-like, they sit attached only by their rear legs to a twig, with the body held rigidly at an angle. Some green ones resemble unopened leaves or buds, and a few eat blossoms and attach petals to themselves. These caterpillars tend to remain motionless during the day, imitating stationary objects. The moths have mottled wings and rest during the day with wings flat against the bark or foliage.

Many caterpillars in this second largest lepidopteran family are very destructive to deciduous and coniferous trees. The well-known cankerworms feed on the foliage of shade, lumber, and fruit trees.

Silkworm Moths
Family Bombycidae

The oriental silkworm *(Bombyx mori)* no longer exists in the wild, but it has been bred in captivity at least since the beginning of written history. In modern times, many genetic strains have been developed for the production of different kinds of silk.

Each female lays several hundred eggs. The caterpillars are fed fresh mulberry leaves daily and mature in about 45 days. The pupal stage lasts only 12 to 16 days. The fat, whitish cocoon, composed of a single thread about 1,000 yards (914 m) long, is unreeled for silk; the pupae are then eaten by the factory workers or sold as a delicacy.

The creamy-white moths are robust and hairy, with a wingspan of about 2 inches (51 mm). These short-lived adults do not feed, and females never fly.

The huge silk industry is based primarily on this species, although there are many other silk-producing moths in other families, a few of which produce commercially usable silk.

▲ Inchworm

▼ Silkworm Moth ▲ Geometrid Moth

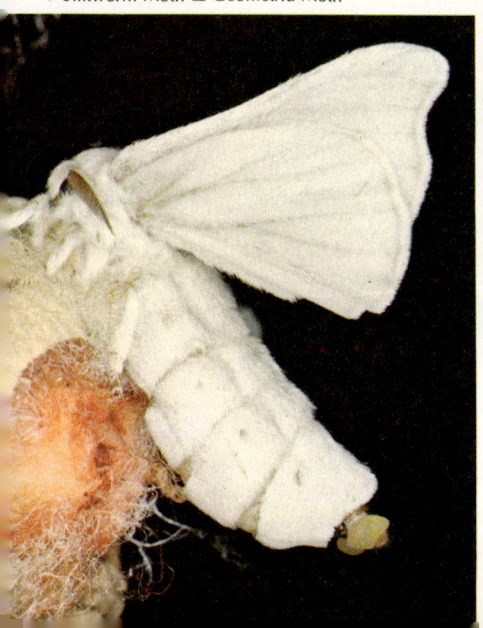

▲ Silkworm larva

103

Tent Caterpillar Moths
Family Lasiocampidae

Tent caterpillars spin extensive, communal webs in the forks of trees and sometimes include much of a small tree. Large areas of orchard or forest trees are defoliated during occasional outbreaks of these caterpillars, and the adults are then attracted to lights in hordes.

The females lay eggs in a ring encircling a twig, and the eggs overwinter and hatch in the spring. The young of one batch stay together and spin their dense web, which protects them at night; during the day, they leave the tent to feed on foliage. Each caterpillar makes a trail of a single silk thread when it leaves the web to feed and returns along that trail to the nest. When large, the caterpillars leave the nest and soon each spins a separate cocoon in a sheltered crevice.

The brown, gray, or reddish adults have stout, hairy bodies and moderate wingspread. The male antennae are feathered. The lappet moths are other members of this family and do not spin communal webs. Their larvae have small lobes or "lappets" on the side of each of their body segments.

Tussock Moths
Family Lymantriidae

The extremely destructive gypsy moth originated in the Old World and arrived in North America in 1869. Female gypsy moths are winged but never fly. After emerging from a thin cocoon attached to a tree, the female moth remains near the hairy shell to await a mate. The eggs are laid on top of the cocoon, covered with brownish hairs from the female's conspicuous anal tufts, and overwinter there. In the spring the tufted, dark caterpillars, with their distinctive bright blue and red markings, hatch out to begin their voracious feeding. The first two larval stages can develop normally only if they choose among a certain 42 species of plants (including willows, birches, and oaks) but the larger larvae can grow successfully while feeding on more than 450 species.

Another European introduction into North America is the browntail moth, whose caterpillars defoliate shade and forest trees and have hairs that irritate human skin. The beautiful white satin moth is a pest of willows and poplars in the northern hemisphere.

▲ Female Gypsy Moth ▼ Male ▲ Larva

Corn Earworm

Noctuid Moths
Family Noctuidae

Millers, owlets, cutworms, and armyworms are some of the names used for members of this family. By far the largest family in the order, it totals about 20,000 species, many of which are agricultural pests in all parts of the world. The adults are medium-sized, robust, and hairy. Dull in color except for a few groups such as the bi-colored underwing moths, many have a dusty look (hence the name "miller"). Most medium-sized moths attracted to lights are noctuids.

The usually smooth caterpillars feed mainly at night on green plants. Some bore into plant stems, others feed under the bark of dead logs. A few prey on scale insects.

An especially destructive noctuid is the corn earworm, which feeds not only on corn but also on tomatoes, cotton, and other crops. It overwinters in the south, then spreads northward each spring, but cannot survive the cold winter in the north. The eggs hatch in about a week and the larvae burrow into the corn ear, tomato fruit, or cotton boll. Pupation takes place in the ground. Only 30 days are required in warm weather for the development from egg to adult. Two generations occur annually in the north, five or more in the south.

Underwing Moths
Family Noctuidae

The most beautiful noctuids in the northern hemisphere are the underwing moths. They rest on tree trunks during the day, their mottled gray or brown forewings blending perfectly with the bark. The brilliant hindwings remain hidden under the forewings until the moths are disturbed; then the bright color is suddenly flashed, probably startling predators enough for the moth to fly away. The hindwings of most species are banded in red or orange; a few are black, yellow, white, or even blue.

The adults hatch in the middle and late summer and live for a few weeks. Females glue the eggs under loose bark; these hibernate, hatching as the food tree leafs out. The larvae grow rapidly and are very muscular: when alarmed some can flip several inches into the air. They have a looping gait like inchworms. Except when very small, the larvae feed only at night and crawl down the tree to hide in litter on the ground during the day.

These striking moths are woodland dwellers, their larvae feeding on deciduous trees or shrubs. Most species eat only one or a few related plants. A flimsy silk cocoon protects the pupa during the short time before the adult emerges.

▼ Adult Tiger Moth ▲ Banded "Woolly Bear"

Tiger Moths
Family Arctiidae

The strikingly handsome tiger moths are favorites of moth collectors, and children are fond of the densely tufted caterpillars, some of which are called "woolly bears" or "hedgehog caterpillars." Unfortunately, the bristles can be dangerous if rubbed into the eye.

Most tiger moths have strongly contrasting color patterns of yellow, orange, or red combined with dark and white spots and stripes. They are highly poisonous to birds and lizards. The larvae frequently have bold patterns, too, such as red and black bands, and curl into a compact ball when disturbed. Some species hibernate as mature caterpillars. Many kinds of plants, even lichens, are hosts of the caterpillars. Pupation takes place in a weak cocoon covered with caterpillar hairs. When the adults emerge, the females remain next to the cocoon, emit a powerful wind-borne sex attractant, and do not fly until mated.

Certain beautiful white arctiids are adults of the webworms, which spin communal webs enveloping a whole shrub or tree branch.

Giant Silkworm Moths
Family Saturniidae

The largest insects in the world (in wing surface area) are the Atlas moth of India, southern Asia, and Malaysia, and its two close relatives in Australia and Papua. Females of these moths can measure as much as 10½ inches (27 cm) in wingspread. Other enormous saturniids include the North American cecropia and polyphemus and the European emperor (all about 6 inches or 15 cm across).

The stout, furry body of saturniids is small in proportion to the broad wings. The virgin females do not fly but emit an aphrodisiac scent, which the broadly feathered antennae of males are able to detect a mile or more distant. Most saturniids are nocturnal but some fly only in daylight.

The large eggs of many saturniids are glued to the leaves of ailanthus, willow, maple, and many other trees, on which the giant caterpillars feed. The caterpillars have brightly colored tubercles, thin hairs, or stinging spines. (The caterpillars with stingers hatch from masses of eggs laid in a ring around a twig.) The dense silk cocoons, loosely closed at one end, are attached to branches or lie on the ground in leaf litter. The silk of Atlas moths has been widely used commercially.

Luna Moth
Family Saturniidae

The lovely vivid-green luna moths, with their long "tails," are collectors' prizes the world over, though they live only in Asia and in North America from Canada south to Nicaragua.

The caterpillar, large and plump, is about 2¾ inches (7 cm) long when fully grown. Its body is greenish and the head either green or reddish, turning mostly green at maturity. The American luna feeds on sweet gum, walnut, oak, beech, birch, and other trees. The cocoon, thinly woven but tough, is spun in a covering of leaves and falls to the ground when the leaves drop.

The adult luna moth is about 4¾ inches (12 cm) long, the tails alone making up half that length. Wingspan is about 5 or 6 inches (12.5-15 cm), and each wing has a small transparent "window." Males have very broadly feathered antennae, females less so.

Pairing takes place in late evening. The dark-brown, white-spotted eggs are laid in small clusters. Two broods appear annually, the first flying in May and June, the second in August.

▲ Bedstraw Hawkmoth

▲ Sphinx caterpillar ▲ Elephant Hawkmoth

Sphinx Moths
Family Sphingidae

When disturbed, the large caterpillars of sphinx moths rear up in a posture supposedly suggesting the Egyptian sphinx but actually more like a threatening cobra. The larvae are also called hornworms because most species have a pointed "horn" on the rear end. Each hornworm feeds alone in broad daylight, exposed on the foliage. The tomato and tobacco hornworms of the Americas are familiar to gardeners as ravenous pests on their tomato and *Nicotiana* plants. Hornworms pupate in earthen cells. In temperate climates there is one generation a year, with the wintering stage always the pupa.

Adult sphinx moths, or hawkmoths, are among the fastest fliers in the insect world, and a few regularly migrate long distances. The wings and body are streamlined, and the thorax is huge and muscular. Like hummingbirds, they hover over flowers and sip nectar with the extremely long tongue, meanwhile carrying pollen from flower to flower. Of the many plants adapted for hawkmoth pollination, the most remarkable is a Madagascar orchid with a nectar spur 12 inches (30 cm) long; a native sphinx moth has a tongue similarly long.

Giant Skipper Butterflies
Family Megathymidae

These butterflies can be distinguished from most hesperiid skippers by their size (more than 1⅝ inch or 40 mm wingspan) and by the lack of a hook at the tip of the antennal club. They are stout, hairy insects with wings in tones of black, brown, or tan, usually with pale markings. They fly rapidly and jerkily, always near the yuccas or agaves in which their larvae feed. The adults do not eat and they live only a few days.

The megathymids are unique among all the world's butterflies in having grub-like larvae that live their entire lives as internal borers, in the underground stems of yuccas or in the thick leaves of agaves. They occur exclusively from the southern United States to Central America.

The large caterpillars of a Mexican species bore into the maguey plant (an agave) and are called "gusanos de maguey." Tequila, the celebrated Mexican liquor, is made from the juice of the maguey and distillers of some of the finer tequilas pop a maguey caterpillar into each bottle as a symbol of quality. The gusanos are a popular and expensive delicacy in Mexico and can be purchased fresh or canned.

Skipper Butterflies
Family Hesperiidae

The 3,000 species of hesperiid skippers all have a hooked tip on the antennae that no other butterflies possess. The thorax is stout and the wings relatively small and stiff. They are rapid fliers and can fly in a straight line, unlike the usual fluttering flight of most butterflies. Skippers are dull-yellow, brown, or blackish, often with light or metallic markings. Wingspan usually measures less than 1¼ inch (31 mm). They are avid nectar feeders and have extraordinarily long tongues.

Differing from larvae of other butterflies, skipper caterpillars have a large head, set off from the body by a slender "neck" (actually the front part of the thorax). During the day the caterpillars hide individually in silk-lined shelters of leaves fastened together or in a rolled leaf. They feed at night, the most primitive species on legumes and other plants, the more specialized ones on grasses (a few are lawn pests), sedges, and palms.

The slight cocoon is made in the larval shelter and anchored by a stem at one end and by a silk girdle. Overwintering can take place either in the larval or the pupal stage.

Orange Sulphur

Whites and Sulphur Butterflies
Family Pieridae

White, yellow, or orange with black wing margins or spots, the pierids abound in sunny fields in the warm months. Various tropical pierids also migrate in swarms for long distances.

Species of white cabbage butterflies are common in Europe and Asia and have been accidentally introduced into North America, Australia, and elsewhere. Their larvae are serious pests of cabbages, broccoli, and other plants in the mustard family. The pretty orange and yellow alfalfa butterflies of North America and Eurasia are pests of alfalfa and clover.

Pierid caterpillars are slender and velvety, without defensive scent glands or spines. They are mainly green, and a few species are gregarious. The pupae are always attached at the tail end by a median silk girdle.

The eyes of certain pierid pupae can perceive the color of their surroundings, and the brain responds by releasing a hormone that changes the color of the pupa to match the background.

Swallowtail Butterflies
Family Papilionidae

Among the largest, showiest butterflies are the papilionids, including the familiar zebra and tiger swallowtails. Most have yellow or iridescent dark colors with vivid markings in contrasting colors. "Tails" on the hindwings are almost universal, and sexual and seasonal color differences are frequent. One fascinating swallowtail is a widespread African species with several female forms each mimicking a different butterfly that is distasteful to predators; the males all look alike and do not mimic.

Papilionids are abundant and varied in the tropics and usually live in forested regions. In jungles of Papua, the East Indies, and Southeast Asia the brilliantly colored birdwings abound.

Pipevines, citrus, parsley, and carrots are a few of the larval foods of various swallowtails. Smooth (except for a few with long, soft filaments on the back), swallowtail larvae often have staring eyespots on the thorax or gaudy stripes and spots. All have a Y-shaped, usually orange, scent organ on the thorax that shoots out when the caterpillar is disturbed. In temperate climates the pupa overwinters.

▲ Tiger Swallowtail ▼ Black Swallowtail caterpillar

Viceroy
Family Nymphalidae

Both sexes of the North American viceroy closely resemble the unrelated monarch butterfly. This mimicry is an advantage to the edible viceroy because experienced birds and other predators mistake it for the poisonous monarch and do not eat it. The caterpillar resembles a bird dropping and eats willow and poplar leaves. It overwinters in a shelter of leaves fastened with silk. There are at least two broods a year.

Another famous nymphalid is the mourning cloak, one of the few butterflies that hibernate as adults; it becomes active on the first warm days of spring. In Britain it is called the Camberwell Beauty.

The front pair of legs in members of this family is reduced to such a small size that they cannot be used for walking, so these insects are remarkable for having become quadrupeds. In all males and some females these legs are clothed with long hairs.

Monarch
Family Nymphalidae

The American monarch is the most spectacular of the few insects that have a true bird-like migration. In the late summer the eastern populations rapidly fly south to the sub-tropics and the California ones move to coastal groves. During the migration and in the wintering grounds the monarchs congregate in thousands on specific trees at night and on cool days. Mating begins in early spring and the eggs are laid on milkweeds during the slow flight northward. When the offspring mature, they continue northward. Several non-migratory generations follow quickly in the summer range. The monarch has reached even remote Pacific islands and now breeds there wherever milkweeds grow.

The monarch and its relatives are large and conspicuous butterflies, unpalatable to birds because their caterpillars store the alkaloid poisons from the leaves of their milkweed foodplants. The caterpillars' bright transverse stripes warn experienced birds to beware. Because it migrates to warm lands during the winter, the monarch is the only one in the group that is able to breed in places where winters are cold.

▲ Viceroy ▼ Monarch coming out of chrysalid

▲ Monarch on Rabbitbrush

Wood Nymph

Satyrs and Wood Nymphs
Family Nymphalidae

Many satyrs and wood nymphs, like their mythological namesakes, inhabit shady woodland glades; others fly in meadows and bushy areas. One group occurs only in high mountains and in far northern regions. Some fly at dusk rather than in daylight.

These butterflies are colored in soft shades of gray, brown, and orange, and are usually decorated with small eyespots. The bases of the forewing veins are often swollen. The velvety, green or brown caterpillars may have a pair of small tails and sometimes head "horns." Their customary diet consists of grasses and sedges; a few species are minor pests on rice, barley, sugar cane, and in oriental countries, bamboo.

The pupa is suspended upside down from a silk pad or lies within a slight cocoon on the ground.

Morpho Butterflies
Family Nymphalidae

The dazzling, iridescent wings of certain morpho butterflies are familiar mounted under glass in trays, picture frames, and jewelry. The splendid color of morphos is structural, so it does not fade as pigmented colors do. Each scale is striated and breaks up the light rays into various wavelengths by reflection and interference.

Morphos soar among the trees in tropical jungles of Central and South America. Many species are blue but some are whitish or brown. The hindwings are depressed along the inner margins where the abdomen rests when the insects are inactive.

Blues, Coppers, and Hairstreak Butterflies
Family Lycaenidae

The upper surface of the wings of these small, delicate butterflies is usually metallic-blue, copper, or green, and so attractive that the wings are made into jewelry. Each hindwing of some lycaenids has a slender, hair-like tail. Meadows, roadsides, and other open areas are the habitat of most of these insects.

Short, stout, slug-like caterpillars, the head and legs almost hidden, are characteristic of the family. Most are plant-feeders (mainly on legumes), but others, the only predacious butterfly caterpillars, eat ant larvae and pupae, scale insects, mealybugs, and aphids. Many lycaenid larvae are ant-guests: they have honeydew glands and are "milked" by the ants. Not all species that live in ant nests feed on the ants; some leave the nest at night to feed on leaves.

▲ Bog Copper ▼ Bog Copper ▲ Large Copper

Hercules Beetle

Beetles
Order Coleoptera

The number and diversity of beetles is awesome: there are already about 278,000 different kinds known! The order is the largest single group of the animal kingdom. Among the insects 40 percent are beetles, which are classified into about 140 families.

Most beetles are easy to recognize: the front wings are hardened into a shell-like or leathery sheath and are called *elytra* (singular, *elytron*). When a beetle is not flying, the elytra cover the hindwings and usually the abdomen and meet in a straight line down the middle of the back. The elytra are not used for flying but swing out to the sides, and the large, membranous hindwings do the work.

Beetles have well-developed chewing mouthparts. Most species go through one life cycle per year, but a few may take up to five years, and some have several generations in one year. In body length beetles range from $1/100$ of an inch to 4 inches (0.25-100 mm).

121

Tiger Beetles
Family Cicindelidae

Brilliant, metallic colors are typical of the flashy tiger beetles, which are closely related to the ground beetles. Unlike many major insect groups, the brightest hues are found on temperate as well as tropical species. These long-legged predators run and fly swiftly while pursuing insects.

The eggs are laid in the soil, and the cylindrical larvae usually live in tunnels or burrows in the ground, moving quickly up and down to grab prey or retreat from enemies. The disk-shaped head with its strong jaws is used as a trap door which closes the top of the burrow. To prevent being pulled out of the burrow by its stronger victims, the larva has a pair of strong hooks on its back to anchor itself. Pupation takes place in the burrow, and the life cycle takes from two to three years for completion.

The smallest tiger beetles are only ¼ inch (6 mm) long, while the largest, in Africa, reach 2¾ inches (70 mm) in length. Most members of the family are between ⅓ and ¼ inch (10-20 mm) long. A few have lost the ability to fly and of these, some are nocturnal, surface hunters, some live in trees and resemble ants, and a few live in termite nests.

Ground Beetles
Family Carabidae

Among the most beneficial insects are the highly predacious carabids, which relentlessly pursue their prey on the ground and even up into trees. They destroy many kinds of small invertebrates, from caterpillars, grubs, and other immature and adult insects to snails and slugs. These heavily armored beetles run but seldom fly and generally hunt in the dark, so naturalists find them under stones, logs, and debris in the daytime. Their favorite hunting grounds are in forests and near water, and they live in most environments, including polar regions.

A distinctly bad odor emanates from many adult ground beetles, emitted in vaporous or liquid form from anal glands. When disturbed, the tiny "bombardier beetles" shoot out, with a surprisingly loud pop, a misty puff of gas.

This large family (25,000 species) has a wide variety of habits, forms, and sizes ($1/12$ to $3½$ inches, or 2-85 mm). Their coloration may be bright and metallic, especially in the tropics, but most are dark. Some species have extremely long heads that enable them to reach into a snail shell and eat the occupant.

Predacious Diving Beetles
Family Dytiscidae

"Water tigers" is the descriptive name given to the ferocious larvae of this family, which will attack anything, even an animal larger than themselves. Their prey is mainly insects but includes even small fish, tadpoles, and salamanders. Sickle-like jaws clamp onto the victim while the larva's digestive juices flow through channels in the jaws into it. The food is then sucked up as a liquid.

The adult diving beetle is almost as insatiable as the larva in capturing prey underwater. An excellent swimmer, using its long, flattened, and fringed hindlegs, surfacing from time to time to gather an air bubble under its elytra, the beetle is able to stay submerged for long periods. It can, to some extent, diffuse oxygen from the water and carbon dioxide into it. An able flier, it may move to new water at night and often comes to lights.

Predacious diving beetles are hard, oval, and smoothly streamlined. Most are dark-colored, often with dull-yellow borders, and the elytra are usually smooth. The largest is 1 5/8 inches (40 mm) long, the smallest less than 1/25 inch (1 mm). The 2,500 species live primarily in the northern hemisphere.

Whirligig Beetles
Family Gyrinidae

Remarkable divided eyes are a hallmark of these boat-shaped aquatic beetles: one portion of each compound eye is located toward the upper surface of the head on each side and the other portion, well separated, lower on the head. When the beetle swims along the water's surface, the upper eyes see above the water line, the lower ones below it.

Whirligigs live on the surface of moving or quiet water but prefer the latter. As their name suggests, they swim rapidly in circles when disturbed, often in large assemblages. Usually active in daylight, they seek floating prey, living or dead. The eggs are laid in clusters on leaves of submerged plants. The carnivorous larvae remain underwater, usually near or on the bottom, and breathe dissolved oxygen through plumy gills. They prey on aquatic nymphs and adults, predigesting them as do dytiscid larvae. When mature, the larvae develop air-breathing organs and leave the water.

The broad, dark body of a whirligig beetle is shiny and smooth, never longer than 3/4 inch (19 mm). Tropical species are often iridescent and brilliantly colored.

▲ Predacious Diving Beetle

▲ Whirligig Beetle ▼ Whirligigs on water surface

Water Scavenger Beetles
Family Hydrophilidae

Like the Gyrinidae, these beetles breathe oxygen while underwater from a stored air bubble under the elytra that is periodically renewed by surfacing, and supplemented by diffusion of dissolved oxygen in the water. In addition, water scavenger beetles carry along a film of air on the underside of the body, giving them a silvery look. When the beetle surfaces to take on a load of air, the hydrophobic club at the end of the antenna breaks the surface film while tilted at such an angle that the outside air flows into the storage area under the elytra.

Though similar in general appearance and size to the predacious diving beetles, water scavenger beetles have short, clubbed antennae. What appear to be long, slender antennae are actually one pair of elongated mouthparts (palpi). The eggs are usually laid singly, often attached to water plants or carried about on the mother's underside until they hatch. Some species spin a silk envelope for a packet of eggs. Adults of most species feed on rotting plant material, fungi, and dung, but some are predatory. The larvae are mostly carnivorous, preying on snails and other easily captured victims.

Rove Beetles
Family Staphylinidae

A flexible abdomen that can curl upward and forward is the most remarkable feature of the rove beetle. This motion helps to fold the hindwings after flight and perhaps is also a threat to predators.

Rove beetles are long and slender and are rapid runners, with short, strong legs. The larvae resemble the adults in color and form and, of course, lack wings and elytra, but are more secretive than the adults. Most species seem to be predators of insects and mites; some live in nests of birds, mammals, or termites; more than 300 species live in ant nests, welcomed by the ants because of their sweet secretions. A few species eat ant larvae but are still tended in all stages by the ants. Other rove beetles eject fluids to repel enemies.

This cosmopolitan family is one of the largest groups of insects, totaling more than 27,000 species. The largest are more than an inch long (32 mm), the smallest only $3/100$ inch long (0.7 mm). Rove beetles can be found almost everywhere, most commonly around or under decaying material.

Carrion Beetles
Family Silphidae

When certain carrion beetles find a small dead animal, they undermine it. Using their forelegs to dig beneath the carcass and their heads to shovel the earth away, they gradually lower the body into a hole, lay eggs on it, and partly cover it. If the carcass is not in a suitable place and is not too large, these amazingly strong beetles will move it a few feet. In this way a moist, abundant food supply is provided for both larvae and adults. In a few species, the food is eaten and regurgitated by the parents for their larvae.

The 1,600 species of silphids include some that are plant- or fungus-feeders or even ant-guests, and a few that are snail-predators, but nearly all are found on decaying flesh.

These are the largest of the beetles found on carrion, usually more than ⅓ inch (10 mm) but ranging from ⅛ to 1⅓ inch (1.5-35 mm) in length. Many have handsome orange and yellow markings, and the body is broad and flattened or elongate and thick. The last four segments of the antenna are fuzzy and enlarged into rounded lobes, much bigger than the rest of the antenna. The short, stout, spurred legs are ideal for the function of digging.

Stag Beetles
Family Lucanidae

A male stag beetle's large, curved, and jagged jaws, which project out for some distance in front of the head, look very dangerous. The formidable appearance is enhanced by the rugged body and elbowed, clubbed antennae. But lucanids, which are chiefly nocturnal, are not predators: the adults do not feed at all or feed only on honeydew, nectar, and sap oozing from tree leaves and bark, and these mandibles are used only in combat with other males.

The 750 species of stag beetles are closely related to the scarab beetles but can be distinguished from them by the inability to close the plates of the antennal club and by the huge mandibles of the males.

Adult stag beetles are convex, elongate, and robust. The body surface is usually brown or black, but tropical species are often beautifully colored. The largest stag beetles are more than 2 inches (50 mm) long and the smallest about $1/5$ inch.

The eggs of stag beetles are laid in crevices in bark, usually near the roots. The larvae are plump and pale and up to 1 5/8 inch (40 mm) long. The life cycle is similar to that of the scarab family.

Scarabs
Family Scarabaeidae

The largest insect (in sheer bulk) is the Goliath beetle of Africa—4 inches long. It is one of the 17,000 species in this family. One familiar kind is the June beetle, a large brown insect that flies to lights in late spring.

The Japanese beetle was accidentally introduced into North America from Asia in 1916 and is now a widespread plant-eating pest. In July or August the eggs are laid in soil and soon hatch; the larvae feed on roots and overwinter in the ground. The life cycle takes one year.

One group of dung-feeding scarabs are called tumblebugs because a pair of them roll a piece of dung into a ball, then, using their hindlegs, one pushing and one pulling, roll it some distance and bury it. An egg is laid in it and the dung serves as a food supply for the larva. To the ancient Egyptians, who considered the scarab sacred, the local tumblebugs' habit of dung-rolling symbolized the earth's turning. The beetle itself was a symbol of eternal life and of the sun-god Creator, the sharp spikes on the beetle's thorax symbolizing the sun's rays. Scarabs were also used as talismans in ancient Rome.

▲ Goliath Beetle ▼ Japanese Beetles

Flatheaded Borers

Family Buprestidae

"Jewel beetles" is a name commonly applied to these insects because many of them have brilliant colors that flash in the sunlight during flight. The beautiful elytra of the larger species are used in artwork and handicrafts, and the whole body of the smaller ones made into jewelry.

This family of 11,500 species is most abundant in tropical forests but is common in cooler areas also. Adults are very active on hot, sunny days and when flying may produce a loud, buzzing noise.

The adult beetles feed on leaves and especially nectar-bearing flowers; a few are fungus-feeders. From eggs laid in bark crevices emerge soft, pale larvae that are blind and legless. The front end of the body is broad and flattened, thus giving rise to the common name of the family.

The larvae bore into dead or dying trees or shrubs—rarely into healthy ones. With their powerful jaws they make galleries under the bark and into the wood, feed, and pupate there, making them serious pests in standing timber and in orchards. Sometimes buprestids emerge from lumber long after it has been made into buildings.

Click Beetles
Family Elateridae

One way to turn over from back to front is to flip oneself into the air. A click beetle achieves this not with the legs but by a unique method: the underside of the front part of the thorax bears a backwardly directed spine that catches against the edge of a socket on the middle part of the thorax. When the spine is drawn off its catch it snaps forcefully down into the socket with a loud click and causes the elytra to strike the surface on which the beetle is lying (upside down), propelling the latter several inches into the air.

These beetles are rather narrow, hard, and long, measuring $1/5$ to 2 inches (3-54 mm). Wireworms—click beetle larvae—live in the soil in great numbers and do tremendous injury to agricultural crops by feeding on the roots. Other click beetle larvae live in rotting wood; some are predators. From two to five years are required for the larvae to mature after hatching from eggs laid in soil, rotten wood, or debris.

The adults of some click beetles eat buds of fruit trees and shrubs. One giant African species lives in termite nests. About 7,000 species of click beetles are known, among them one group of about 100 species in the American tropics that are luminous, like firefly beetles.

▲ Adult Click Beetle ▼ Wireworm

Soldier Beetles

Family Cantharidae

The hunting grounds of these close relatives of the firefly beetles are flowers and foliage. Most prey on small insects, such as aphids and mealybugs, while a few eat only pollen and nectar. The brightly contrasting color pattern (yellow, orange, or red on a dark background) brings to mind a soldier's parade uniform and this may have been a reason for their common name. They are sometimes called leather-winged beetles because of the soft elytra.

Soldier beetles, of which almost 3,500 species are known, resemble firefly beetles in appearance, except that the head is not concealed and, on the average, these beetles are a little smaller. They are not luminous.

The velvety, dark larvae of most species are predacious, feeding on soft-bodied insects, such as caterpillars and maggots, and on insect eggs; a few are omnivorous and eat plants as well as insects.

Fireflies or Lightning Beetles
Family Lampyridae

One of the delights of a summer night is the pattern of tiny flashes of light from fireflies. The light varies from green to yellow to red in different species. It comes from a substance called luciferin, which is found in glands in the last few abdominal segments of either sex at any stage. In the presence of the enzyme luciferase and air, the luciferin oxidizes, giving off light but little heat. The insect can control the amount of oxygen that reaches the luciferin, so it can control the duration and rhythm of the flashes. Each species has a characteristic rhythm, and in the adult beetles this is a courting signal.

Less than 4/5 inch (20 mm) long, fireflies have highly contrasting color patterns, such as black and orange, and are distasteful to birds. Females, although often winged, may not fly. Those of many species look like larvae and are called glowworms.

Although the family of 2,000 species is primarily tropical, they are common in temperate regions, especially in humid places. During the day they rest on vegetation; at night the larvae search for food—insects, snails, crustaceans, and earthworms—which is partially liquefied by digestive juices before being imbibed. The adults do not feed.

◀ Adult Carpet Beetle
▼ Larva

Dermestid Beetles
Family Dermestidae

Tiny beetles that dine at our expense on high protein diets are dermestids. They eat animal products, such as wool rugs and upholstery, furs, leather, silk, woolens, and dried meat and cheese, and also infest unprotected specimens in natural history museums. These scavengers can completely devour the flesh of a dead animal, leaving only the skeleton—an ability exploited by zoologists who maintain colonies of dermestids in tight containers to clean specimens of vertebrates. In the wild, dermestids are scavengers and carrion-feeders. Adults of many smaller species are found on flowers eating pollen and nectar. Some dermestids live in mammal, bird, bee, or ant nests and feed on organic debris. A few species are pests in granaries.

The antennae of dermestids are short and clubbed. The body is compact, oval, convex, and less than half an inch (12 mm) long. The adults are usually dark, but some are patterned with colored hairs or scales, and the larvae are brownish and very hairy. It is the larvae of the house and museum species that do most of the damage, and their shed skins may often be seen in closets and under rugs. In buildings they breed continuously all year.

Blister Beetle larva

Blister Beetles
Family Meloidae

"Spanish fly" (cantharidin) is a chemical obtained from the dried bodies of certain European and Asian blister beetles and was used for more than 2,000 years in human and veterinary medical practice, externally as a blister-causing counterirritant and internally as a diuretic and aphrodisiac, sometimes with fatal results.

The blister beetles have a rather elaborate life cycle: masses of minute eggs are laid in the soil, often near the egg sites of ground-dwelling host insects. The larvae are parasitic on either grasshopper eggs or the immature stages of bees. First-stage larvae have good legs and are very active in getting to their hosts. The bee-parasites climb up plants and wait on flowers until a bee comes along, then attach themselves to it and hitch a ride to the bee's nest, eventually feeding on the eggs, larvae, and pupae, as well as on stored honey and pollen. Soon after reaching their hosts, blister beetle larvae become legless, sluggish grubs.

Most adults of the 2,000 kinds of blister beetles feed on plants, although a few do not feed at all. Some of the adults are crop pests. The usual size of meloids is about ⅜ to ⅝ inch (10-15 mm) in length.

Darkling Beetles
Family Tenebrionidae

The well-known "mealworms" that are fed to pet birds, mammals, and reptiles are larvae of one kind of darkling beetle. The mealworm is reared commercially in huge numbers for this purpose, but when it occurs naturally, it can be a serious pest in granaries, mills, and warehouses. The adult is a blackish beetle about ⅝ inch (15 mm) long.

The scientific name of this family comes from the Latin *tenebrio*, meaning "one who loves darkness," and refers to the nocturnal, secretive habits of its members. Few are good fliers: most live on the ground beneath stones or rotting logs, or in termite, ant, or bird nests.

The 15,000 species in this family are varied in appearance, but all have a hard body, a dark color (some with white or red markings), long legs, and a small head. Many are wingless or have the elytra fused together. Their sizes range from $1/12$ to $1⅜$ inches (2-35 mm).

Tenebrionids are mostly scavengers, feeding on decaying vegetation, dung, fungi, or stored grains and cereals.

▲ Darkling Beetle larva
◀ Adult

Lady Beetles
Family Coccinellidae

Ladybugs or ladybirds, these small beetles are a favorite kind of insect in song and folklore around the world. So it is satisfying to know that most of the 5,000 species are also beneficial in their eating habits, devouring great quantities of soft-bodied plant pests. One outstanding example is the Australian lady beetle that was imported into California in 1892 to control a plague of citrus scale insects and probably saved the industry in what was the first case of planned biological control of an insect pest, a practice now widespread because it is both effective and non-polluting.

Mites, thrips, aphids, scales, mealybugs, and whiteflies are the favorite food of many lady beetle adults and larvae. The diets of certain other species include manure, spores of mildews and rusts, pollen, and leaves. The leaf-feeders include some crop pests, such as the bean and squash beetles, but these are far outweighed by the usefulness of the majority of the family.

Lady beetles feign death when alarmed, dropping off the foliage and remaining motionless. When attacked they also exude from body pores and leg joints a toxic, repulsive fluid that is dangerous if taken internally.

Longhorned Beetles
Family Cerambycidae

The astoundingly long antennae are this family's most characteristic feature. These tactile organs are slender and usually longer—sometimes several times longer—than the body.

Longhorns are found in forests everywhere. The adults eat bark, flowers, leaves, and pollen, though a few are non-feeders. The eggs are laid in or under bark or in cracks in wood or in holes chewed by the female. The whitish, almost or totally legless grubs bore into trees or shrubs and are an important food for woodpeckers. North American aborigines considered the grubs a great delicacy, and both white and brown peoples in Australia ēat them.

The fifth largest family of beetles, the Cerambycidae include about 20,000 species. Many are strikingly colored in metallic or enamel-like hues, especially in the tropics. Certain longhorns mimic the appearance of other insects, such as bees, wasps, ants, bugs, and certain bad-tasting beetles.

Leaf Beetles
Family Chrysomelidae

The Colorado potato beetle is one of the most famous and destructive members of this family and has an interesting history. It probably originated in Central America, whence it spread northward into the Rocky Mountain area, feeding only on the leaves of wild species of nightshade *(Solanum)*. But when the potato (a domesticated species of *Solanum*) was taken westward by settlers in the mid-19th century, the beetle became a serious pest on it and then spread eastward to the Atlantic coast. In this century it invaded Europe and is now a problem almost everywhere that potatoes are grown.

Among the 20,000 species in this family are many other economically detrimental insects, the adults of which eat leaves and the larvae either leaves or roots.

Most leaf beetles are smooth and brightly colored; some tortoise beetles have a striking metallic luster, and others are so attractive that they are made into jewelry. Small to moderate in size, they have various shapes. The larvae also show many forms and may have well-developed legs or none at all.

Weevils

Family Curculionidae

The size of this family is awesome. By far the largest family in the animal kingdom and more than twice as large as any other beetle family, it contains about 60,000 named species, all with a distinctive "snout." The snout is usually longer than the main part of the head, and in certain species exceeds body length. At the tip of the snout are the mouthparts. The antennae, usually elbowed, are attached to the snout and are club-tipped.

Weevils are often dark in color, many with a covering of minute scales or hairs. Some tropical kinds are brilliantly iridescent. Body length varies from minute ($1/25$ inch, or 1 mm) to large (2 inches, or 50 mm). Most are winged.

Many weevils are extremely damaging pests of garden, field, orchard, and timber crops and stored grains. The cotton boll weevil, one well-known example, was originally a native of the New World tropics; it moved northward and is now one of the most important insects in cotton-growing areas of the western hemisphere. The larvae feed and pupate in the cotton boll, hibernate for the winter, and mature the following spring. Other species of weevils infest other kinds of plants as well as fungi and stored grains in all parts of the world.

▲ Boll Weevil ▼ Acorn Weevil ▲ Rose Weevil

▼ Galleries under bark of Ash log

Bark Beetles
Family Scolytidae

Bark beetles create interesting patterns of tunnels and galleries just under the bark of healthy, dying, or dead trees and shrubs. The female excavates one or two main tunnels and lays her eggs individually along its sides. When the minute, legless larvae hatch, each one starts its own gallery at right angles to the main tunnel, without crossing the galleries of adjacent larvae. Each larva finally pupates in its own tunnel and the adult later emerges from the tree. When finished, the tunnel pattern from each group of eggs looks like a huge, long-legged centipede, the details of which are usually characteristic of each species.

Bark beetles are minute (ordinarily less than 1/8 inch, or 3 mm long), hard, and cylindrical. Many members of this family of 7,000 species are serious economic pests, such as the elm bark beetle, a European species, now common in the United States, that carries the Dutch elm disease, a malady that has almost eliminated the native American elm. Another is the coffee-berry beetle, a pest of coffee trees and stored coffee beans. However, coniferous forests sustain the greatest amount of damage from bark beetles.

Strepsipterans mating in abdomen of Bee ▶

Twisted-wing Insects
Order Strepsiptera

With females that spend their entire lives as parasites in various insects, and males parasitic as larvae but free-living, vigorous fliers as adults, the tiny strepsipterans are a curious and rarely noticed lot. Their name describes the twisted, club-like form of the male's forewings, the hindwings being large, clear, and fan-shaped. The adult males resemble certain small beetles. They have bulging, raspberry-like eyes, short antennae with leaf-like sections, and weak mouthparts.

Females are sac-like, blind, and have no appendages. The winged male mates with a female while she is protruding slightly from the host. She has an opening near the front of the body for insemination and for the exit of the new larvae, which hatch inside her. The larvae disperse over the soil and vegetation and try to find a new host insect to burrow into. When they find one, they molt into legless grubs and grow by absorbing nutrients from the host's fluids. Molting and pupation take place inside the host.

Each species of Strepsiptera is a parasite of one or a few kinds of bees, wasps, crickets, bugs, katydids, leafhoppers, planthoppers, or silverfish.

Bumble Bee

Wasps, Bees, and Ants
Order Hymenoptera

A huge order (almost as big as that of butterflies and moths), the Hymenoptera on the whole are beneficial because of their pollination of flowering plants and their predation and parasitization of arthropod pests.

Hymenoptera means "membranous wings," and these insects have two pairs, the hind ones smaller and hooked to the front ones near the base. Other characteristics are the more-or-less narrow waist (actually the first segments of the abdomen) and the large ovipositor, which, depending on the group, is used for sawing or stinging (for defense or anaesthetization of prey) as well as for laying eggs.

Hymenoptera have abrupt (four-stage) metamorphosis. All larvae except those of the sawflies are legless and live as parasites or in food-laden cells prepared by the adults.

This is the only insect order in which all males come from unfertilized eggs and thus have only half the usual number of chromosomes in each body cell. Being fatherless, they inherit only their mother's traits. This condition is found elsewhere among certain scale insects, whiteflies, thrips, mites, and in one species of beetle.

◀ Adult Sawfly
▼ Larva

Sawflies
Superfamily Tenthredinoidea

Like moth caterpillars in appearance and feeding behavior, sawfly larvae have a distinct head with chewing mouthparts, legs on thorax and abdomen, and tiny, simple eyes; but unlike caterpillars, they have legs on the first two, as well as other abdominal segments, and these legs are not tipped with tiny hooks.

The adults are stout and compact; the waist is not conspicuously narrow. The name sawfly arose from the sawing done by the female's ovipositor to cut slits in foliage and twigs for egg-laying. Pupation of sawfly larvae takes place in a silken cocoon in the ground. The pre-pupae overwinter without shedding the larval skin and then molt the next spring. Normally there is one generation a year, and some sawflies take two or more years to develop.

The larvae are leaf-eaters, miners, or borers. (The latter two no longer have legs.) Many sawflies are pests of fruit and lumber trees and ornamentals, and the spruce and larch sawflies of the northern hemisphere are noted devastators. The cherry, or pear, slug occurs almost worldwide as an important defoliator, and the tiny birch leaf miner is a major horticultural pest.

Ichneumon Wasps
Family Ichneumonidae

This enormous family parasitizes insects and spiders. Each species of ichneumon wasp attacks only a few particular kinds of hosts—moth and butterfly caterpillars are favorites.

With the aid of the long ovipositor, the eggs are deposited on or in the eggs, larvae, or pupae of the host, even when the host is in an egg-sac, cocoon, or tunnel. The strong ovipositor can penetrate as much as half an inch (13 mm) into a tree trunk. Very few ichneumons are able to sting humans, however.

The wasp larvae feed externally or bore into their host and feed inside. When mature the larvae pupate in a cocoon in or near the dying host. Ichneumons commonly overwinter as adults.

Usually large and slender, these wasps are often brightly colored in metallic or highly contrasting hues with antennae that are long and straight. Some produce a loud, buzzing noise by rubbing the minute bristles on the forewing against lobes on the thorax.

▲ Gall Wasp on Oak bud   ▲ Wasp gall on Joshua tree

Gall Wasps
Family Cynipidae

The tiny gall wasps insert their eggs into the young tissues of buds, leaves, stems, or roots of plants. In response to secretions of the larvae of most cynipids, the affected plants produce abnormal growths called galls. One or more larvae feed, develop, and pupate in the gall.

Most commonly these galls are on oaks, but some are on plants in the rose and composite families. Each species of wasp produces a gall of a certain shape, size, and color on a particular part of one kind of plant. For example, wild roses form spiny, spherical galls when one species of wasp oviposits on it. "Oak apples" are walnut- or apple-sized galls of another kind of wasp. Gall wasps are not serious pests, and, in fact, the galls were formerly used as a source of tannic acid and dyes and are still so used by pharmacists.

Usually dark, shiny, and with flattened sides, the gall wasps measure ¼ inch (6 mm) or less in length. Some of the species have alternate generations of sexual and non-sexual (parthenogenetic) offspring, and these generations make different galls at different sites on the host plant.

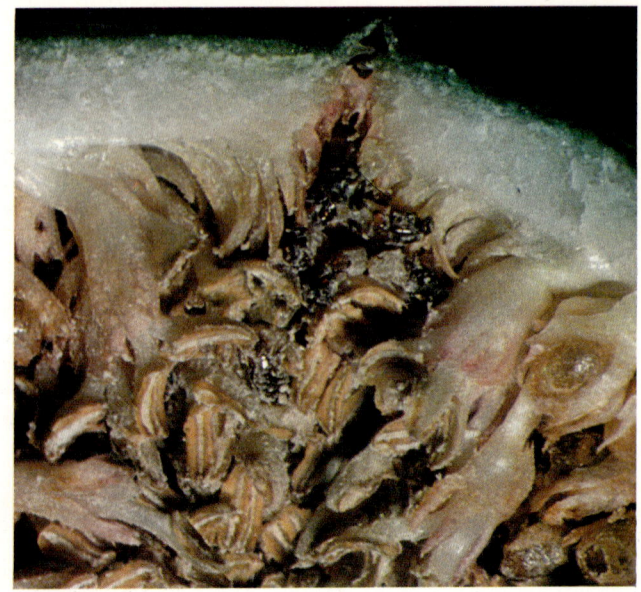

Fig Wasps in Fig

Fig Wasps
Family Agaontidae

The Greek root of the name Agaontidae means "to be wondered at," a name that certainly applies to the amazing life history of these tiny wasps. The production of edible Smyrna figs is entirely dependent on one kind of fig wasp, the blastophaga. Its immature stages live in hidden galls in flowers of an inedible wild fig that produces profuse pollen. The pollen coats the body of the female blastophaga as she emerges from the fruit as an adult. When she flies to the Smyrna fig flowers and tries to oviposit, the pollen brushes off onto them but their structure prevents egg-laying there. The Smyrna fig must be cross-pollinated and the blastophaga accomplishes it. To make it easier and surer for the wasps, fig growers hang flowering branches of the wild fig in orchards of the Smyrna.

The male is wingless, blind, and smaller than the female. Its only function is to fertilize the female's eggs just before she emerges from the gall. The male then spends the rest of his existence in the gall while the female pursues an active life.

Spider Wasps
Family Pompilidae

"Tarantula hawks" are among the most spectacular wasps, with shiny blue-black bodies, orange wings, and large size (up to 2 inches or 50 mm long). In a life-and-death struggle with a tarantula, the slender wasp usually wins by paralyzing the huge spider with its sting. The wasp transports the spider to its previously dug burrow and lays its eggs on the prey. The sting seems to have antiseptic properties that keep the prey fresh for weeks, so the larvae have a suitable food supply on which to develop.

Although spiders are the usual prey, occasionally pompilids use a cricket, roach, or other insect. Some of the wasps do not dig a burrow but sting a spider in its own lair and lay an egg on it. The spider may be only slightly anaesthetized, regaining consciousness and leading an active life for a while with the wasp larva feeding on it. The larva pupates in the spider's burrow.

Spider wasps are not social and do not build communal nests.

Velvet Ants
Family Mutillidae

Strikingly colored in combinations of black with bright red, orange, yellow, or white, the densely hairy velvet ant females are easily recognized. Though ant-like, the wingless females are actually wasps. The velvety coverings may be short or very long and tufted. Velvet ants are able to sting ferociously; large ones are called "cow killers"—an exaggeration, since the sting is not fatal. Mutillids are most common in hot, semi-arid regions. One large group is entirely nocturnal and is plain amber-brown instead of vividly colored. Both sexes are stout and hard-bodied. Males commonly differ so much in color, as well as in having normal wings, that specialists have often named the two sexes as separate species by mistake.

These wasps are fairly large, especially the females; the latter may be 1 inch (25 mm) long or longer. They produce a squeaking noise by rubbing one abdominal plate against another.

Female velvet ants run around seeking burrows of ground-dwelling bees and wasps (rarely flies or beetles), where they lay their eggs on the host larvae. The wasp larvae feed on the host and later emerge from a host's cocoon.

Velvet Ants: ▲ Ecuador ▼ California

Yellowjackets and Hornets
Family Vespidae

A colony of yellowjackets (hornets) is composed of a few queens (fertile females), workers (sterile females), and at times males, living together in a large, enclosed nest of papery material (wood chewed and mixed with saliva). Some species suspend the nest from a branch but most species nest in an excavation in the ground.

In temperate climates the colony dies each winter except for the overwintering young queens, who found new colonies in the spring. Rarely does a queen use an old nest: she usually starts in a new location. The first brood (workers) enlarge the nest and take over all the work; the queen becomes just an egg-layer. The larvae are tended carefully and fed nectar, insects, and other meat that is partly crushed by the workers. Through spring and summer only workers are produced but in the fall both sexes emerge and mating occurs.

The adults eat nectar, honeydew, and juices of fruits and meats. They are dangerously aggressive and can inflict painful stings in defense of their nest.

The larger *Polistes* wasps have a smaller colony and the nest is open and suspended from a slender stem usually under eaves, rock ledges, or in shrubs.

Hunting Wasps
Family Sphecidae

Mud dauber wasps are plasterers. Each solitary female scoops up blobs of mud with her mouthparts from the edges of puddles, ponds, or streams and makes many flights to a protected site under a bridge, eave, or overhanging rock ledge to build a mud nest. The nest will have several cells side by side, each up to an inch (25 mm) long. Each cell is then provisioned with several spiders paralyzed with venom, and the female lays one egg. The larva feeds, grows, and pupates in the cell.

The related digger wasps excavate a nest in the ground or use old tunnels in timber and stow away several paralyzed grasshoppers or caterpillars in each burrow. Experiments have shown that they have a remarkable ability to memorize the topography around the nest.

Sphecid wasps are very choosy about their prey—each species uses only one kind of food for its larvae. Roaches, sawfly larvae, springtails, thrips, and aphids are among those hunted. To avoid carrying prey long distances, each wasp usually builds its nest near the prey's habitat and aggressively defends its own territory. The adult wasps eat nectar, honeydew, and juices oozing from ripe fruit.

▲ Mud Dauber Wasp ▼ Digger Wasp

Leafcutter Bees
Family Megachilidae

These medium-sized, hairy bees have a characteristically large head and are darker and more robust than honey bees. They are solitary insects: each female seeks, for her exclusive use, an abandoned burrow made by another insect in the ground or in rotten or seasoned wood. With sharp jaws she quickly cuts neat ovals and circles of rose or other leaves for use in lining the sides of the burrow. Each cell is stocked with a pollen-nectar mixture, an egg is laid in it, then sealed with a leaf circle. Each burrow is divided into about a dozen cells placed end to end.

Some species of megachilid bees line their nests with other materials, such as thistledown, cotton, resin, or pebbles.

On the underside of the abdomen, female megachilids have brushes to accumulate pollen. Some of the pollen comes off as the bee visits successive flowers, and so these bees are valuable pollinators for many plants, including alfalfa.

Honey Bees
Family Apidae

Cave paintings in Spain show that humans have collected honey since ancient times. The honey bee *(Apis mellifera)* is among the most valuable of domesticated animals, not only for its honey and wax but even more for its pollination of plants.

These insects live in highly organized colonies, each with one queen (a fertile female), 50,000 or more workers (sterile females), and some males (drones), produced at certain times. The workers attend to all non-reproductive activities: secreting wax, building the nest, tending young, gathering pollen and nectar, and making honey. They sacrifice themselves to sting in defense of the hive; the barbed stinger, left imbedded in the enemy, is ripped out of the worker's body, and she is fatally injured. Females live long lives, for insects, and have remarkable learning ability.

The egg-laying queens are reared from larvae fed a special rich food called "royal jelly." From time to time new colonies are formed by a swarm (a queen and workers). Honey bees overwinter in the hive, mainly quiescent, subsisting on stored honey.

Bumble Bees
Family Apidae

The large, heavy-bodied, black-and-yellow bumble bees are primarily adapted to cool climates; many live in high mountains and near the Arctic Circle, and only a few reach the tropics. Though closely related to the honey bee, their annual life cycle is more like that of yellowjackets in that only the young fertilized queens survive the winter. In the spring each queen starts a new colony, usually in an old rodent burrow in the ground. She constructs wax cells, stocks them with pollen and nectar, and lays her eggs on the pollen. The first brood of workers, when mature, take over all tasks except egg-laying and building the egg cells, which become the queen's sole activities. The workers fill the nest with many cells for the growing grubs and for food storage. Most nests eventually contain 100 to 400 workers by late summer. Then only males and fertile females are produced and these leave the nest and mate. As winter arrives, the fertilized females (new queens) hibernate in hollow logs or other shelters, and the old queen, workers, and males all die.

As pollinators, bumble bees are extremely valuable. With their long tongues they can reach the nectar even in cupped flowers.

▲ Bumble Bee on Thistle
◄ Close-up

Carpenter Ants

Ants
Family Formicidae

The most successful of social insects, ants have extraordinary diversity, abundance, and distribution. Already over 10,000 species are known. Their castes include one or a few queens, numerous wingless workers (sterile females), and at times, males. In larger colonies, the workers may be divided into soldiers, nurses, builders, and food gatherers.

With most ants, about once a year each colony produces fertile adults of both sexes, which swarm out in a mating flight. The males soon die, and each mated female sheds her wings and tries to start a new colony. She feeds the first brood of larvae with secretions through her mouth; when mature, these workers tend her and the later young. A few ants, such as the Pharaoh's ant, a common pest species, have no mating flight, and new colonies are formed by a batch of workers carrying young.

Most ant nests are in the ground, but some are up in plants or trees. The giant carpenter ants carve galleries in wood but don't eat the wood. Many kinds of food—animal and vegetable, living or dead—nourish different kinds of ants. All ants can bite and some can sting.

▲ Raid column of soldiers and workers

▲ Queen, soldier, and workers

Army Ants
Family Formicidae

The marauding army ants of the tropics travel in columns, seizing and skeletonizing the animal life in their path. In the best-known American species the columns have no regular leaders: a few workers at a time forge ahead slightly, lay chemical trails, then return to the horde, as others take the lead. The column, flanked by huge-jawed soldiers, moves at most 220 yards (200 m) in a day, camping each night in a sheltered site. This bivouac is formed as a dense mass of half a million or so interlocked ants, with the queen, immatures, and any males in the center. The raiders are only workers and soldiers, all blind; the larvae are moved from one bivouac to the next at dusk, the queen soon following. After two nomadic weeks the colony becomes sedentary. Soon the queen lays 100,000 to 300,000 worker eggs in a short period. When these hatch the colony again starts traveling, hauling along the larvae. When the larvae are pupating, the colony settles down for three weeks. This alternation continues through the year, except for the brief annual production of males and new queens, which leads to the founding of new colonies.

Index

A
alderflies, 63
alfalfa butterflies, 114
Angoumois grain moths, 97
antlions, 64, 66
ants, 144, 156, 157
aphid lions, 65
aphids or plantlice, 61
Argentinian cactus moths, 100
army ants, 157
armyworms, 106
assassin bugs, 51
Atlas moths, 109

B
backswimmers, 46
bagworm moths, 95
bark beetles, 142
barklice, 42
bed bugs, 49
bee flies, 79
beetle mites, 13
beetles, 121
birch leaf miners, 145
bird lice, 43
birdwing butterflies, 115
biting midges, 75
black flies, 75
black widows, 16
blister beetles, 136
bloodworms, 73
blow flies, 87
blues, 120
boll weevils, 141
bombardier beetles, 123
booklice, 42
bot flies, 90
browntail moths, 105
brown widows, 16
buffalo gnats, 75
bumble bees, 155
butterflies, 92

C
cabbage butterflies, 114
caddisflies, 91
Camberwell Beauty, 116
cankerworms, 102
carpenter ants, 156
carpet moths, 94
carrion beetles, 128
casemaking clothes moths, 94
cecropia moth, 109
centipedes, 22
cherry slug, 145
chewing lice, 43
chiggers, 13
Chinese mantises, 32
citrus whitefly, 60
clearwing moths, 96
click beetles, 132
clothes moths and allies, 94
codling moths, 99
coffee berry weevil, 142
Colorado potato beetle, 140
coppers, 120
corn earworms, 106
cotton boll weevils, 141
crane flies, 71
crawlers, 63
cutworms, 106

D
daddy-longlegs, 12
dampwood termites, 30
damselflies, 28
dance flies, 80
darkling beetles, 137
darning needles, 28
deer flies, 76
dermestid beetles, 135
digger wasps, 152
dobsonflies, 63
doodlebugs, 66
dragonflies, 28
drosophila flies, 84

E
earwigs, 35
electric-light bugs, 47
elm bark beetles, 142
emperor moths, 109
European corn borers, 100

F
fig wasps, 148
firebrats, 26
fireflies, 134
flatheaded borers, 131
fleas, 69
flesh flies, 88
flower flies, 82
froghoppers, 57
fruit flies, 83

fulgorid planthoppers, 58

G
gall midges, 76
gall wasps, 147
ghost moths, 93
giant roaches, 29
giant silkworm moths, 109
giant skipper butterflies, 112
giant water bugs, 47
glowworms, 134
goldenrod gall moths, 97
Goliath beetles, 130
greater wax moths, 100
greenhouse whiteflies, 60
green lacewings, 64, 65
ground beetles, 123
gypsy moths, 105

H
hairstreaks, 120
harlequin bugs, 53
harvestmen, 12
hawkmoths, 111
hedgehog caterpillars, 108
hellgrammites, 63
Hessian flies, 76
honey bees, 154
hornets, 151
hornworms, 111
horse flies, 76
house crickets, 39
house flies, 85
human body lice, 43
humpbacked bristletails, 24
hundred-leggers, 22
hunting wasps, 152

I
ice crawlers, 34
ichneumon wasps, 146
inchworms, 102
Indian meal moth, 100

J
Japanese beetles, 130
jumping plantlice, 59
jumping spiders, 19
June beetles, 130

K
katydids, 39

L

lace bugs, 52
lady beetles, 138
ladybugs, 138
lanternflies, 58
lappet moths, 104
leaf beetles, 140
leafcutter bees, 153
leafhoppers, 57
leaf insects, 40
leatherjackets, 71
leatherwinged beetles, 133
lerp insects, 59
lice, 43
lightning beetles, 134
longhorned beetles, 139
long-legged flies, 81
luna moths, 110

M

mantises, 32
mayflies, 27
mealworms, 137
mealybugs, 62
medfly, 83
midges, 73
migratory locusts, 37
millers, 106
millipedes, 21
mites, 13
monarchs, 116
monkey spiders, 17
morpho butterflies, 119
mosquitoes, 72
moths, 92
mound-building termites, 30
mourning cloak butterflies, 116
mud dauber wasps, 152

O

orb-weavers, 18
oriental rat fleas, 69
oriental silkworms, 103
owlets, 106

P

peachtree borers, 96
pear slugs, 145
periodical cicadas, 54
Pharaoh's ants, 156
pink bollworms, 97
pillbugs, 20
plant bugs, 50
planthoppers, 58
plantlice, 59
plume moths, 101
Polistes wasps, 151
polyphemus moths, 109
predacious diving beetles, 124

R

red spider mites, 13
red widows, 16
roaches, 29
robber flies, 78
rove beetles, 127

S

satin moths, 105
satyrs, 118
sawflies, 145
scale insects, 62
scarab beetles, 130
scorpionflies, 68
scorpions, 11
seventeen-year cicadas, 54
shield bugs, 53
silkworm moths, 102
silverfish, 26
skipper butterflies, 113
snakeflies, 67
snout beetles, 141
snowfleas, 23
social bees, 154
soldier beetles, 133
sowbugs, 20
sphinx moths, 111
spiders, 15
spider wasps, 149
spittlebugs, 57
springtails, 23
spruce budworms, 99
stable flies, 85
stag beetles, 129
stink bugs, 53
stoneflies, 36
sulphur butterflies, 114
swallowtail butterflies, 115
swifts, 93

T

tachina flies, 89
tapestry moth, 94
tarantulas, 17
tent caterpillar moths, 104
termites, 30
thirteen-year cicadas, 54
thrips, 44
ticks, 14
tiger beetles, 122
tiger moths, 108
tiger swallowtails, 115
tortoise beetles, 140
treehoppers, 55
tsetse flies, 87
turkey gnats, 75
tussock moths, 105
twintails, 24
twisted-wing insects, 143
two-winged flies, 70

U

underwing moths, 107

V

velvet ants, 150
viceroys, 116
vinegar flies, 84

W

walkingsticks, 40
warble flies, 90
wasps, 144
water scavenger beetles, 126
water striders, 48
water tigers, 124
webbing clothes moths, 94
webspinners, 41
webworms, 108
weevils, 141
whirligig beetles, 124
white ants, 30
whiteflies, 60
whites, 114
wireworms, 132
woodlice, 20
wood nymphs, 118
wood ticks, 14
woolly bears, 108

Y

yellowjackets, 151

Z

zebra swallowtails, 115
zorapterans, 32

Add to your
KNOWLEDGE
THROUGH
COLOR

(All Books $1.45 Each)
(Where marked • $1.95 Each)

The opposite page lists the currently available and constantly growing books in this new paperback series. To add to your KNOWLEDGE THROUGH COLOR library simply list the titles and mail to:

BANTAM BOOKS, INC.
Dept. KTC-1
666 Fifth Avenue
New York, N.Y. 10019

Add 25¢ to your order to cover postage and handling. Send check or money order — please! We cannot be responsible for orders containing cash.

— *A Free Bantam Catalog Available Upon Request* —